Toward Solomon's Mountain

A scene from *A Phoenix Too Frequent*, in a production by the Fairmount Theatre of the Deaf, located in Cleveland, Ohio. Photo by Deborah S. Workman.

Toward Solomon's Mountain

THE EXPERIENCE OF DISABILITY IN POETRY

*Edited by Joseph L. Baird
and Deborah S. Workman*

Temple University Press
PHILADELPHIA

Temple University Press, Philadelphia 19122
© 1986 by Temple University. All rights reserved
Published 1986
Printed in the United States of America
The paper used in this publication meets the minimum requirements of American National Standard for Information Sciences—Permanence of Paper for Printed Library Materials, ANSI Z39.48-1984

Library of Congress Cataloging-in-Publication Data

Toward Solomon's mountain.

Bibliography: p.
Includes index.
1. American poetry—20th century. 2. Physically handicapped—Poetry. 3. Physically handicapped, Writings of the, American. I. Baird, Joseph L. II. Workman, Deborah S.
PS595.P58T68   1986   811'.54'080355   86-4426
ISBN 0-87722-416-1

This book is lovingly dedicated to Gram McFadden and Edward and Hazel Workman

If my legs cannot move

I will wriggle my toes

Till they learn

to do intricate dances.

    LILLIAN MORRISON

Contents

"If my legs cannot move . . ."
    LILLIAN MORRISON   v

Acknowledgments   xv

Toward Solomon's Mountain   1

I

JAMES WEIGEL, JR.
   Testaments: I, V, XXVI, XXVIII, XXX   13
   A Farewell   17

MARY R. GAUMOND
   Virus Poliomyelitis   18
   The Rose   19

DIXIE PARTRIDGE
   Angles   21
   While Pruning   22
   At Nuclear Medicine   23

HAROLD BOND
   The Game   25
   Dancing on Water   26
   Detour   27

JAN GLADING
    Arthritis   29
S. L. FRIEDMAN
    On Seeing a Construction of a Sheet Metal Man   30
SUSAN L. DUNN
    "Tonight I stood looking. . . ."   32
    "Today, again, the jagged
        black line. . . ."   32
    "They are all too kind. . . ."   33

II
NEDINE DAVIS
    I Am Mama Bear   37
MICHAEL BACHSTEIN
    Clinics   38
    Terms of Surrender   39
    My Name in the Star Registry   40
JOHN MANN ASTRACHAN
    Jenny   42
LILLIAN MORRISON
    On the Sidelines   43
SHARON A. STERN
    reawakening   44
    kol nidre   45
    bitter herbs   46
    talisman 18   48
MARILYN DAVIS
    Song for My Son   49
    The Changeling   50

EDWARD L. HOOPER
I Know, You'd Rather Be Dead 52
The Way Downtown 53

III

NORMAN ANDREW KIRK
Crip 57
Black Aggie 57
The Tingle 58
ROBIN GATHANY SHEA
"Caught behind words..." 60
"Don't smile..." 61
GLORIA MAXSON
Enid Field: In Memoriam 62
Two Guitars 63
NEIL MARCUS
"Zotz!" 65
Disabled Calligraphy 66
JOHN CROSSON
Cripple in Sight 67
JANICE TOWNLEY MOORE
At the National Air and Space Museum 68
CONSTANCE E. STUDER
Reflections 69
Suspension 70

IV

NORMA THOMAS COLVIN
On Forgetting to Cry 75
Cowboy-Boot Sale 76

VIVIENNE FINCH
   The Journey   77
   On Being Stone   79
   An Earthquake Somewhere Else   81
DEBORAH KENDRICK
   For Mama   92
   A Question of Art   93
   Me and Hercule Poirot   94
LAURIE STROBLAS
   How to Sign   97
FREDERICA GOLDSMITH
   Capes   98
EVELYN THOMAS
   Covering All Bases   99
JACK HAND
   Pain Is My Brother   100
   Death Stairs/Life House   101
   Pain   104

V

ZANA
   broken   107
AMBER COVERDALE SUMRALL
   A Question of Energy   108
   Mirage   109
   Questions   110
MICHAEL CLEARY
   Fingers, Fists, Gabriel's Wings   112

H. N. BECKERMAN
  "To: The Access Committee..." 113
  Adjustments   114
WILLIAM D. CRAGO
  "... where late the sweet birds sang"   115
VASSAR MILLER
  Subterfuge   116
  Spastic Child   117
  Sampson   117
  Dramatic Monologue in the Speaker's Own
    Voice   119
FELIX POLLAK
  Reality   121
  Tunnel Visions   123
  The Finger   125
  Incident   127

Biographical Sketches of the Contributors   129

Select Bibliography   143

Author-Title Index   145

Index of First Lines   147

Thematic Index   149

Acknowledgments

Debts of appreciation have accumulated in the four years or so that this book has been in the making. We want to especially acknowledge Mimi Dane, who was with this work from the beginning, giving enthusiastic support and encouragement at a most crucial time. We are especially grateful too to James Curtis Moe, psychologist, friend, and sensitive reader, who provided a fine sounding board for the poems as they came in. Professors Bobby Lee Smith and Clyde W. Jentoft, both of Kent State University, gave early and continuing support by their appreciative commentary on the poems that they read at various times. We are also indebted to the following people for putting us in touch with poets that we otherwise might have missed: Carson Heiner, Editor of *Kaleidoscope*; Brad Chaffin, Editor of *Joyful Noise*; Samuel Miller, former Editor of *Disabled Writers' Quarterly*; C. J. Lampos, Editor of *Achievement*; Mary Johnson, Editor of *The Disability Rag*; Florence Ludins-Katz and Elias Katz, Directors of the Institute of Art and Disabilities; Dr. Alice P. Kenney of the National Access Center; and Marsha Saxon of the Boston Self Help Center, who read Rumi's "Longing for the Birds of Solomon" over the phone, long distance from Boston. Appreciation is also due to the following friends and supporters: Vera Buk, Emil Sattler, James Wuille, Gary Hubbell, and Eve Baird.

Our especial appreciation goes to Robert Bly and to Yellow Moon Press for permission to use Mr. Bly's translation of Rumi's "Longing for the Birds of Solomon," first published in the volume *Night and Sleep* (Brighton, Mass.: Yellow Moon Press, 1981).

We also wish to note our great appreciation to the Office for Research and Sponsored Programs, Kent State University, for support in the form of a summer research grant and a grant-in-aid for miscellaneous expenses.

Finally, we want to thank the many individuals and publications for granting permission to reprint those poems that have previously appeared elsewhere:

John Mann Astrachan, "Jenny." First published in *The New England Journal of Medicine*, May 27, 1982. Reprinted with permission.

H. N. Beckerman, "Adjustments." First published in *Achievement* 14, no. 2 (1982). Reprinted with permission.

Harold Bond, "Dancing on Water." Originally appeared in *Poetry Northwest*, Fall, 1968. Reprinted with permission from *Dancing on Water* (Omaha, Neb.: The Cummington Press, 1970), copyright 1969 by Harold Bond.

Harold Bond, "Detour." Reprinted with permission from *The Way It Happens to You* (Saddle Brook, N.J.: Ararat Press, 1979), copyright 1979 by Harold Bond.

Harold Bond, "The Game." Originally appeared in *The Young American Poets* (Chicago: Follett/Big Table Books, 1968). Reprinted with permission from *Dancing on Water* (Omaha, Neb.: The Cummington Press, 1970), copyright 1969 by Harold Bond.

Michael Cleary, "Fingers, Fists, Gabriel's Wings." First published in *The Texas Review*, Fall/Winter, 1983. Reprinted with permission.

Nedine Davis, "I Am Mama Bear." First published in *Joyful Noise* 2 (1981). Reprinted with permission.

Frederica Goldsmith, "Capes." First published in *Kaleidoscope* 11 (1985). Reprinted with permission.

Edward L. Hooper, "I Know, You'd Rather Be Dead" and "The Way Downtown." First published in *The Disability Rag*, Nov. 1983 and Aug. 1983. Reprinted with permission.

Deborah Kendrick, "For Mama," "Me and Hercule Poirot," and "A Question of Art." First published in *Kaleidoscope* 6 (1982), 9 (1984), and 10 (1985). Reprinted with permission.

Norman Andrew Kirk, "Crip," "Black Aggie," and "The Tingle." First published in Norman Andrew Kirk, *Some Poems, My Friends* (Boston: Four Zoas Night House, 1981). Reprinted with permission.

Vassar Miller, "Spastic Child," "Subterfuge," and "Dramatic Monologue in the Speaker's Own Voice." Reprinted by permission of Latitudes Press, publisher of *Vassar Miller: Selected and New Poems, 1950–80* (Austin, Tex.: Latitudes Press, 1981).

Lillian Morrison, "If my legs cannot move . . . ." First published under the title "The Old Hoofer" in *Who Would Marry a Mineral* (New York: Lothrop, Lee and Shepard, 1978), copyright 1978 by Lillian Morrison. Reprinted by permission of the author.

Lillian Morrison, "On the Sidelines." Reprinted by permission of the author.

Dixie Partridge, "Angles" and "While Pruning." First published in Dixie Partridge, *Deer in the Haystacks* (Boise, Idaho: Ahsahta Press, 1984). Reprinted with permission.

Felix Pollak, "Reality," "Tunnel Visions," "The Finger," and "Incident." First published in Felix Pollak, *Tunnel Visions* (Peoria, Ill.: Spoon River Poetry Press, 1984). Reprinted with permission.

Robin Gathany Shea, "Caught behind words . . ." and "Don't smile . . . ." First appeared in *The Disability Rag*, Oct. 1982. Reprinted with permission.

Constance E. Studer, "Suspension." First appeared in 1978 in

Big Breakfast, a literary magazine published by the University of Colorado. Reprinted with permission.

James Weigel, Jr., "Testaments" and "A Farewell." First appeared in *Kaleidoscope* 9 (1984) and 11 (1985). Reprinted with permission.

Toward Solomon's Mountain

A decade ago this anthology would have been impossible; two decades ago inconceivable. It is, in fact, sobering to realize that only at this point in history could there have been produced a volume of serious, tough-minded poetry wholly concentrated upon the experience of disability. This volume is truly, in a very large sense, *aliquid sub sole novum*, "something new under the sun." It is not, of course, that poetry on this subject has never been written before; on the contrary, one is tempted to remark, there has been far too much: sentimental, saccharine verse produced by disabled writers out of the stereotype thrust upon them by "normal"—that is to say, non-disabled—society, or inauthentic work by "outsiders" who project their own simplistic sentiments onto an experience completely foreign to them. All very well intentioned, of course—and all quite uninteresting. Only in the last few years, apparently as a result of increasing political involvement, including the drive for equal educational and accessibility codes, have disabled people gained, not so much the capacity for getting beyond the stereotypes—the majority have always had that—but the ability to view themselves and their own peculiar experience with a new kind of objectivity. They have, in short—to rephrase the old paradox—achieved the personal distance necessary for the creation of good, intensely personal poetry. And it will become clear to the reader, we believe, that the poetry gathered here fully authenticates that new spirit abroad in the land.[1]

    1. The pre-eminent voice of this new spirit among disabled people is the acerbic little magazine published out of Louisville, Kentucky, entitled *The Disability Rag*. The very title itself, with its aggressive assertiveness, speaks volumes. In the early days of publication, in fact, the heady, confrontational air

That new spirit, however, was a long time in coming, and the changes on the literary level, when they have come at all, have come very quietly, unobtrusively.[2] Almost totally unknown to the general public (and even, indeed, to the disabled community itself) a body of high-quality poetry devoted to the theme of disability has been quietly growing up over the past few years. Published in special anthologies, daily newspapers, or magazines directed primarily to disabled people themselves, these poems have gone largely unremarked. And yet in their simple, sparse delineation of tangled, complex feelings, and their penetrating glance at humanity from a startling, oblique angle, they should have earned the attention of a far wider audience.

The neglect, however—indeed, the positive rejection—of such poetry is hardly surprising. For suffused as the subject of physical impairment has become (certainly in western culture) with emotions of supersentimentality, self-pity, and superficial sympathy, it is scarcely to be wondered at that such a theme has been branded as *verboten* by the canons of good taste. Yet one cannot help wondering whether this attitude

---

implied by the title called forth some little dissension, apparently, from the readers and, perhaps, even from the editorial staff, for the magazine was published for a brief period, somewhat apologetically, under the bland title of simply *The Rag*, with *disability* consigned to oblivion. Happily, the braver spirits won out in this confrontation, and the full title was soon restored. *The Disability Rag* is, it seems clear, both a product of the new attitude among disabled people and a powerful force in giving form and direction to that attitude.

Moreover, the large number of disability journals of high quality that have come into existence in just the last few years is, we think, significant. In addition to *The Rag*, there is *Coping*, an outspoken, politically oriented journal published in New England; *AADC News*, published by the notable, new American Association of Disability Communicators; *Word from Washington*, a tough reporter of the political scene; and even a farm magazine, *Breaking New Ground*, published out of Purdue University and directed to the rural disabled community.

2. The rest of this paragraph and the following one draw heavily upon J. L. Baird, "En-Abled Poetry," *Kaleidoscope* 7 (1983): 33–35. This article was subsequently reprinted in *Mainstream* and *Rehabilitation Digest*.

does not speak to some deficiency in our own sensibilities. For the theme, in and of itself, is no less "poetic" than the other frailties of the human condition, and it, too—like any "normal" literary theme—can speak the language of wry humor, quiet desperation, white-hot anger, robust comedy, bleak despair. Moreover, as will become clear in the following pages, such poetry, by its very nature, grounds itself in hard, concrete, physical fact, and, at its best, achieves that quantum leap that, without diminishing or negating, distances the fact and discloses the spirit in a rare and unusual way.

But why, one might still ask, why an entire volume of poetry devoted to this particular theme? And the answer comes immediately: why indeed not? Why not, since the very language we use is saturated with pejorative, disabling images ("the *blind* leading the *blind*," "*crippled* by the political climate of the time," etc., etc.); since the literature we read is peopled with skewed representations (oscillating wildly between Tiny Tim and Captain Hook);[3] since the drama we watch—and in particular the recent spate of "inspiring" TV melodrama—is awash with simplistic (not to say, simple-minded) exaggerations (from the stickily romantic *Butterflies Are Free* to the bitter, and embittered, *Whose Life Is It Anyway?*).[4] Why indeed not? It is time we heard the real, the authentic voice.

3. See *Pity and Fear: Myths and Images of the Disabled in Literature Old and New* (New York: International Center for the Disabled, 1981). This little booklet is composed of papers delivered at a literary symposium sponsored by the International Center for the Disabled in collaboration with the United Nations on 27 October 1981. Of especial interest is the lead article by Leslie Fiedler, "Pity and Fear: Images of the Disabled in Literature and the Popular Arts."

4. See Jeanne W. Zingale, "The Disabled as Taboo: An Examination of Physically Disabled Characters in Twentieth Century Plays Produced in New York City," Ph.D. diss., Kent State University, 1984. As the abstract notes, this study undertakes "to demonstrate through selected plays that twentieth century playwrights express the attitude that physically disabled persons are taboo and that although there has been some amelioration of that perception in recent years, the disabled are still not seen as normal human beings or accept-

That voice is, at times, admittedly a bit strident in its new sense of itself. The audacious little *jeu d'esprit* entitled "Zotz!" by California poet Neil Marcus, for example, impishly flaunts its vocal inabilities while giving full, clamorous voice to a kind of extended, uninhibited exclamation. This deliberate, sputtering, tongue-tangling poem, which paradoxically demands oral recitation for the full flavor of its utterance, speaks with unaccustomed and unselfconscious abandon.

As Marcus says, "kind of n.e.w. thing.EMERGing" here: a damburst of long-pent-up feeling, without restraint. What is so startling about this piece is the poet's insistence on being heard *in his own voice*, his refusal (even in the cloaking medium of print) to "pass": I sputter; therefore, I am. We may not like it, we may even be repelled by it, but we are forced to reckon with it.

For sheer audacity, however, Marcus' second piece of nonverbal eloquence, called simply "Disabled Calligraphy," can scarcely be topped. With bemused self-detachment, the writer quietly constructs a deceptively simple picture-poem accompanied by a seemingly uninspired label. The reader takes it all in at a glance: the picture, the label, and, unexpectedly, the raucous, jeering laughter of the poet reverberating somewhere in the background.

This kind of black humor and disregard for traditional poetic form will not, of course, be to every reader's taste. But the range here is very wide. William Crago, for example, invokes the most hallowed poetic tradition in English literature in his skilfully crafted ". . . where late the sweet birds sang." Pulitzer prize nominee Vassar Miller speaks to the oppressive, unconsciously condescending attitudes that one invariably encounters, with her finely etched lines:

---

able in roles demanding intimacy or work." See also Lauri Klobas, "Here's Lookin' at You: TV's Concept of People with Disabilities," *The Disability Rag*, Jan.–Feb. 1985, pp. 3–6, and Klobas, "Phys Diz Showbiz: TV's Kids with Disabilities," *The Disability Rag*, Aug. 1985, 21.

> Of course, you are not (I would not accuse you of)
> thinking of holding me down, but of holding me up

and

> I'm either a monster
> in search of a horror movie to be in,
> or else I'm a brain floating within a body
> whose sides I must gingerly touch while you glance
> discreetly away.

And to all those (Elizabeth Bouvia *et al.*) who think disability a fate worse than death, Edward Hooper, in his "I Know, You'd Rather Be Dead," provides his own sharp rebuke with his nicely absurd image of himself gaily wheeling into the grave, "needing but two pallbearers."

Not all of the poems collected here, however, are by disabled writers, and that fact represents a conscious decision on our part. For we felt that such work would give a perspective, otherwise unattainable, on just how much perceptions have generally broadened and expanded in the last few years. At times, however, the distinction was, surprisingly, difficult to make from the simple fact of the poem alone. A poem such as Robin Gathany Shea's "Don't smile . . . ," for example, demonstrates a depth of understanding that is really quite remarkable, and I must confess that this particular editor was taken aback to discover that it was the work of an "outsider." From the poem itself one would have no inkling that Ms. Shea (who, it is interesting to note, gained her insight by work with the disability rights movement) had herself never experienced the destructive, demeaning forces that she delineates so well. Other poems are more obviously from an outsider's point of view, such, for example, as Michael Cleary's "Fingers, Fists,

Gabriel's Wings," chosen for the particularly vivid expression it gives to the experience of watching the graceful movements of American Sign Language, or Marilyn Davis' stark little poems from the mother's perspective. In a few instances, it should be noted here too, the editors have included poems that range somewhat beyond the immediate governing theme, simply in order to round out the selections from a given writer.

In the past few years, the disability movement has effected radical changes in the areas of legal rights, accessibility, educational and employment opportunities, and, most notably, modes of perception; and, as is usual with such shifts of consciousness, these changes are having their inevitable impact on the literature of the culture. This present volume is eloquent witness to that impact. The poetry here is detached, separate, self-contained; it is not about disability rights or indeed "about" anything that might be so precisely specified. Yet it can, we believe, in some sense be said that the disability rights movement has wrought no change more significant than that illustrated by the highly crafted poetry contained in the following pages. To gain the detachment necessary for such creativity, to learn to view oneself with such clear-sighted objectivity, to play the alchemist with such raw, leaden material—*that* is no mean accomplishment.

Some seven centuries ago the Sufi poet Rumi wrote the poem which has provided the title for this anthology, and with that poem, without further comment, we bring this introduction to a close:

Longing for the Birds of Solomon

Is this Stuff poetry? It's what birds sing in cages.
Where are the words spoken by the birds of Solomon?

How would you know their cries, if you heard them,
when you haven't seen Solomon even for two seconds?

That bird lifts his wings, one tip touches East, one West.
Those who hear the note feel an intensity in their whole
    body.

The bird descends from the Holy One's bedroom door to
    earth,
and from earth it flies among light back to the Great
    Seat.

Without Solomon every bird is a bat in love with
    darkness.
Listen, oh mischievous bat, try to become his friend—do
    you want to stay in your cave forever?

If you go even three feet towards Solomon's Mountain,
others will use that as a yardstick to measure their lives.

If your leg is gimpy, and you have to hop, what's the
    difference?
Going there, even by limping, the leg grows whole.

J. L. B.

I

JAMES WEIGEL, JR.

from Testaments

I.
The egg grew human
tracing evolution's dark route
in the womb.
                Luck
seemed to abscond afterward
as coordination slipped
haywire. My strange form
worked poorly to far worse.
                Control
loosened: more limits.

Now thirty-seven, wheelchaired,
    tense,
a small man with crooked spine
and thick speech,
genetically futile, I watch
a universal erosion
of bodies—
            grandparents
changed to dust
and spirit; my parents lapsing
into idleness, dissatisfied
with the mirror.

Time rumples me, too.

Yet I must live the soul's life
pastured, transcendent
in the bone. This dying flesh
was lent to me
                like light.

v.
Translated once
from sex to life,
I entered daylight
to be transformed again,
frog prince of sorts
with stricken nerves.

Love alters me
into my truest shape
but avails no fresh
or conjugal future.
I eat others' wedding cakes.

I would slip
this glove of body off—
humped, bony, sweated, sore—
except the weary thing
shows where I live.

Not flesh but spirit
is hard to cope with;
quicksilver streaking out.

It might go anywhere, attach
to any radiant woman.
I love by omen.

XXVI.
I should quit this craft—
leave it to ladies
with numinous names,
to blotchy adolescents pining
for free sex, or men of talent
who make games with words,
and an odd genius here and there.

Sawdust dribbles from my tropes.
I can't hide it.
Difficult to alter this grating verse
or my stagnant cravings.
It's harder still to bow my head.

The first person singular
is a tic of mine, a nervous reflex
to a sheet of paper. The typewriter
lures this illness to crisis.

Damn! Must I repeat
the shadow-boxing lunacies
of youth in middle age?
An *I*'s a rotting tooth.

XXVIII.
Out of my sleeves ten bones protrude—
two Reaper's paws. Fisted,
they gesticulate not to stress words
but point some object, pat
a dog or rake an itch.

Lean prongs like these
will never coax a breast to swell.
They manage barely fork
and typewriter. A hunt and peck
concern, my fingers forego much else.

Still, these hands work
at a vocation which, by plying
an alternate relax and wrench,
discovers bone-truth.
      And past
my small self
these knobby spires point,
palm to palm, above.

XXX.
A mouth should launch words gracefully,
but my tongue lolls in its bed
like a terminal patient.
      Something wrong
in the brainstalk, some motor harm,
makes this voice rumble and hum,
an irregular bass. I speak the English

of a vacuum cleaner, while
the thread of meaning breaks in my jaws.

Perplexity ripples your face
as the noises explode; my features strain
to get those noises out. Annoyance
and sympathy entice us to laughter.
Yet your ears transpose my raw primeval speech
into a different range, where I am understood.

A Farewell

While time hustled
out of my cancerous
grandmother
her bone hand pawed
the air like an antenna
of some crushed
insect.
The fine
drugged soul floated
on ether as
the X-ray fingers shook
in protest and waved
that galvanic goodbye.
The rest of us twitched
for months at the loss.

MARY R. GAUMOND

Virus Poliomyelitis

You sent me, God,
a microscopic
angel.

How omniscient!

Had it been larger,
I'd have shot it down
with RAID

and would now
be dancing
in the moonlight

with
   Satan.

The Rose

Dawn peeled mists
like tired backing
from mirrored panes
and the common morning
revealed its commons:
the wind crossed maple,
the naked thrust
of the mountain ash

        and a rose.

Warmed by fall vagary
the rose had budded,
a wet curl of red
upon November thorns,
and the woman at the
window responded. The man
moved by ancient memory
brought November's offering
and laid it at her hand.

        coffee brewed.

She curved two petals
to a tolerable raft

and set the resurrection
of the rambler's summer
on water.

        "Come thaw,"
he promised, "I'll feed
the roots and prune
the vine."

"The scent is faint—"
She leaned above. A wisp
of hair slid down,
shut out his view.
With fingers awkward
now to mores of love
he tucked the strand
behind her ear.

They sat
drinking bitter brew
waiting for the rose

        to open.

DIXIE PARTRIDGE

Angles

Gram died with most of her joints frozen
At right angles. My childhood watched
Her form brittle until she couldn't walk;
After that her frame assumed unchosen

Angles of the wheelchair and cracked like deadwood.
When I see my father now, I feel
A bloodrush back: his spine congeals
From the hips a rigid angle forward.

As in some half-forgotten dream
I've lived a future; it persists
In hard lumps on my wrists,
A bamboo gait and a grip growing lame.

Here where I live the trees grow at a slant
To northeast with the wind; they calcify
In traction. Across from my early
Years, trees grow straight along the ditchbank,

Each shaped like an ostrich feather.
Enchanted child, I think they've volatile
Powers to create the wind as they will
By fanning still air.

While Pruning

What tree would shape itself like this?
Symmetrically stocky, branching out wide
a foot above the earth, its center opening
to sun. Harvesting will be within reach.

Perhaps we learn from the haphazard—lightning,
disease, hungry deer in winter—to cut cleanly,
paint to seal the wounds.
Gram used to say *leave them be*

when we wanted to prune the lilacs
crowding her yard path.
Each year arthritis calcified more knots
into her joints, decreed

her movements painful, brittle,
restricted to the house and to the porch
where she sat with her lilacs for sun.
They stretched around her, shielding

the skeletal eighty pounds, knees that would not
unbend, hands that would not open.
My aunts would offer
there'll be more blossoms

if we cut them back . . . but no one pruned
at all until after she died.
We have to duck those lilacs even now
to get to the porch when we visit my father.

He allows them whatever space
they reach out for.

At Nuclear Medicine

Waiting Room
They have met here before: five old women
and a man who arrives feebly
on the arm of his daughter. One wears accumulating
baldness with a yellow scarf; one smokes incessantly;
one sits apart—an Indian woman in purple,
face stoic but eyes alert. They are joking,
asking after common things—cats and the weather—
their church-toned voices separate
from reception efficiency of typewriters, personnel.

I wait for a diagnostic scan and wonder
if they schedule these elderly together—
an exclusive social club.
A nurse comes in, waits
for a pause in conversation. Then,
her hand on a shoulder like a blessing,

says "your turn," lightly
as a hairdresser might. There is silence
until they have gone.

Sanctum
I am led through heavy doors.
Across the room, a woman in a hospital gown
sits high on a table, white hair radiating
from her head in a baroque halo.
She stares into space, her feet jerking
rhythmically, and will not look at me.
Placed in a curtained cubicle, I wait.

I witness for the ritual
I have intruded upon—the low voices,
whirs and clicks removed from me
by design of a grey-striped curtain.
Later, I am brought in my gown
by attendants in baby-blue lead aprons
to the center of the room. There,
mounted in massive stainless steel,
the eye of a god.

HAROLD BOND

The Game

You are my friends. You do things
for me. My affliction is
your hangup. It is yours more
than it ever could be mine.
You spread my affliction thin

enough to go around once
for all of us. You put my
coat on for me when I ask
you. You put my coat on for
me when I do not ask you.

You embrace my shoes with your
compassion. You tell me I
would be less apt to fall with
rubber soles. You carry things
for me. You tell me they are

heavy things, how it would be
difficult for anyone
to carry them. You open
mustard bottles for me. You
tell me how hard it is to

open mustard bottles. I
agree with you. I will not
destroy our game. At night I
dream I am Samson. I will
topple coliseums. I

will overwhelm you with my
brute power. I will knock you
dead. I will open mustard
bottles for you. I will show
you how easy it really is.

Dancing on Water

Mothers who clutch the hands of your children,
what fable can I claim to assure you
these are not drunken sealegs I walk on?
If there is an unseen line I follow

woozily down a winter street, this is
the only act of faith I know. You walk
distances around me, winging like hens
protectively over your broods. I take

these intricate steps only in the dance
I do. I balk gravity by timing
the one disjointed knee that will collapse
predictably as a jackknife. Something

is special in the way I walk, sealegs
to be sure but drunken only in what
blue waters will not buoy me up. These rags
of kneebones for my fable, can we not

call it beautiful that I move over
such fathoms in this my clumsy fashion?
We will say I am dancing on water
in my faith. Ladies, I must dance or drown.

Detour

The road was straight up to the last.
At last the wind rose to meet us.

Who were these strangers calling our names,
these roadrunners at each curve?

Burma Shave signs dotted the way,
but there was no comfort in words.

Distance became our constant lover.
The journey was an end to itself.

We saw stucco houses in ruins,
air clogging our throats like sawdust.

Where, O where did the world go?
Geography no longer was a game.

It lasted as long as November.
Sleep beckoned to us with empty arms,

yet we could not enter that embrace.
The only exit was the one we passed.

The throttle sputtered, and clouds of smoke
beleaguered the terrain in our view.

All we could see was a warm cave,
and we were back where we had started.

JAN GLADING

Arthritis

damn:
ache
again
in
that
place
the
hands
can't
reach,
that
"No,
Jan!"
land
across,
between
the
shoulder
blades,
that
goddam-
made
off-limits
land
made

just
to keep
pain in.

S. L. FRIEDMAN

On Seeing a Construction of a Sheet Metal Man

You tell me somewhere
a great dream was lost

fallen from the sky
in its ambitious flight

that you were reconstructed
from its battered wings

and that you cried:

    Mind, accomplice
    whose mysterious fingers

    carved out hieroglyphics
    of the past,

    let not the barren light
    wipe my eyes bare.

    Wind, rise in my eyesockets,
    stir Quiet's metal cheek.

Oh, I would engage you
with the colors of my soul

but all I have is
this riveted shape

this caricature that states
Man himself is what
the machine grinds.

once, I was subject
for philosophers

but now am a model
for engineers

although if you look close
within a guarded aperture,

a timorous, stunted prisoner
peers out.

SUSAN L. DUNN

"Tonight I stood looking..."

Tonight I stood looking at what I knew was a starry sky, trying to think that at night, I miss little—for little is seen and so much is felt. But something is missing, thinking of evenings short months ago when I had taken in this time. I miss the stars most of all, their brilliance hidden from me now. Yet I commune with the night, breaking the bitter moon's wafer and sipping the heavily purpled wine of the sky.

"Today, again, the jagged black line..."

Today, again, the jagged black line appears in my field of vision. But as my eyes move and dart to focus, it moves and darts away. Sometimes there is a sudden shower of pepper-like flecks. Once the scar-like line took the shape of a bird. Like the warped body of a great black bird, it appeared and heralded the dawn. Other times, unseen, it casts its shadow, grey and swelling across the dusk. I wonder what keeps this creature airborn, ever free of earth. I am jealous of its freedom and hate it, knowing this messenger of night hovers in wait for me.

"They are all too kind . . ."

They are all too kind and all so gentle, guiding my steps in my lateness and darkness. Even kind so far as a kiss, meant somehow to heal and not hurt as it does.

II

NEDINE DAVIS

I Am Mama Bear

Watching me approach, Goldilocks asks,
    "Can I sit in your chair?"
She climbs aboard my albatross—
    Wheels herself away
    Her delight gives that dead bird
    the gift of earthbound flight
    "It is too big. I have to grow—
    it was fun to try."
My chair is rejected for its size
I wish everyone had Goldilocks' eyes.

MICHAEL BACHSTEIN

Clinics

When I am four a crippled hospital
Peels me out of my parents' arms
To make me better. I wring my mother's neck

For safety, knowing this is not
What they said would happen, that they
Are as unnerved as I am to see
Their mangled only son stripped from their love
Into the cracking-plaster bowels
Of this place, into a row of endless cages
Where children no stronger than their parents'
Worst fears lie writhing, waiting for the legs

The doctors have promised. I have made it
Perfectly clear ever since breakfast
That I want to stop there again on the long
Way back, at that same roadside place
Where I slurped up my hungry hot oats this morning
And they said we'd be sure to, but now
They just stand there growing smaller as some
White-headed woman with her glasses on a chain
Around her neck takes me down the long green
Hallway frowning, and they are still waving goodbye
As we turn the ugly corner and disappear, and what
If I never get my legs and they forget me?

Terms of Surrender

Unhappy childhood, please do not curve
Back to the skull of that city
Where the smallest of our straining efforts
Were sequestered by fools, and I shall not remind you
Of all the little centuries you let my love

Down. Let's not go back to dirty streets
Where rival children's insults rippled
In exhaust fumes, or retrace steps that led us
Past eyes that didn't know the meaning
Of a crutch, the sanity of language
Twisted sideways by nerves; no, let us
Merely feel sorry for ourselves and be

Older. It is better this way, as liquor-numbed
Suns go down on our silence and leave the world
A toy to be forgotten, and we fool
Our foolish memory with charades of good humor
And lust, and forget the tiny minds that had us
Boxed into a world of smaller circumference
Than the forward tires of a rolling chair. Truth,

The wicked trail you wind to the center of my sleep
With your calls for resolution will not
Corrupt me into thinking I can change, I am too good
At being crippled to scare myself with any

Shock of ambition, though I know even now
I am better than the double-bent image that hangs
Around my mirror and never moves, not even to lift
Its dust-encrusted jean knees from the crawlspace.

My Name in the Star Registry

With my luck,
They would find a crippled nova
Somewhere that flares
Into brightness for a day
And a half and then
Peters out, and call it

After me. My immortality
Would thus be reduced
To the blue gas of a dying burner
With no one around to relight
The pilot, and all I would get
For my toll-free phone call
And reasonable fee
Would be a darkness
I could have conjured by

Myself, replete with notarized registration
And astronomical charts
To tell me where I'm not

To be found. My system
Would probably be a happenstance
Of unlivable planets circling
Hank Aaron or Sinatra, with me
Just a groundless rumor of quivering light
On the naked horizon, another drunken poet
Making an ass of himself, disappearing
Into the gas of real existence.

JOHN MANN ASTRACHAN

Jenny

You see it's that she can't remember songs
and when friends come to play and want to sing,
you know, songs that children always sing,
she can't remember the songs she sang
even the day before, songs all children sing.

She plays with younger ones,
one little girl really,
and she is so much quicker than my child
and screams at her and calls her stupid
because she can't remember songs.

She can ice skate,
there's nothing wrong with her balance,
and so she glides and looks sad and bewildered
at those who can both skate and sing,
songs that all children know and sing.

And when she is older and the songs are harder
and she needs songs to sing
if she is hurt or loves or isn't sure,
what will she do;
my child who can't remember songs.

LILLIAN MORRISON

On the Sidelines

If I ransom my injuries
with poems
will my joints harmonize?
muscles, in the act of singing,
embrace them?
Will torn ligaments marry
and support me
in moving toward you?
Perhaps if my words are strong
I, too, will be,
knowing again
the marvelous mute scrimmages.

SHARON A. STERN

reawakening

the old german nurse
huge robust woman
tells me to get fresh air everyday
she will not tell me of the foul air
she once breathed and perhaps produced.

everyone is hung and strung up
i too am coming unglued
and search for a new better paste
a finer kinder fixative
to fuse myself and face you.

i who yearn for spring
was born in october
and give birth to myself
new conception
every fall.

kol nidre

'i missed you at services last night.'
yes i couldn't make it, i mumble.
'i'm sure there was a good reason.'
yes i went crazy yesterday.
is that a good reason.

i am having trouble with synthesis
again. my style is changing but meanings
do not meld and are merely juxtaposed.
i suppose that bluest blue jay knows why;
and i no longer lust for connection.

'we are today,' sing the youngsters.
and what am i. last week maybe.
yesterday i too felt like today.
watching the pope on the tube.
t.v. does make strange bedfellows.

i respond so keenly to chords of cadence
but you hear those hidden subtle themes
long before i do. the pubescent girl
sings the 'shma' loudly and with fervor.
why do you thank me to death.

you are broken and i emerge the strong one,
a one eyed king in the land of the blind.
piety and prurience flower together.
john paul ii and yom kippur soften us
just enough for the long night ahead.

bitter herbs

bitter herbs
salt water, saline
normal saline solution
tears and herbs
normal solution . . .

no.
no normalcy,
no solution . . .
no fruit of the vine
bitter or other . . .

only bitter herbs
dipped in ageless tears,
the inescapable image.
so obvious, the eternal truth
in salt.

how could i have missed it?
and this
the rhythm of my vision
that i must dance with you
no matter what the cost,

in blood my blood
some say integrity
but hell
i am already shattered
and bled dry of weeping.

talisman 18

your words haunt me in the night.
you tell me she is dying,
we are all dying,
and i speak of final acceptance
having read all about it
and you don't quite get it.

how can you quite get it
living seeing through it
while i have only read
and cannot comprehend
the finality of the count.
your words her death.

the weight of your words
wanes with turgid time.
i found this pretty card.
it will not lengthen her life
nor forestall her fear.
but i will clumsily send it.

MARILYN DAVIS

Song for My Son

a wooden puppet with tangled
strings   he bobs and bounces
in mid-air   head flopping
arms waving   my hands
under his arms sustain
his spastic stiffness
the Blue Fairy cradling
sweet Pinocchio

He loves to rock and roll
feet prancing   a crazy
puppet dance   his face glows
with the light   of the wishing
star   and borrowing his
brilliance   we too dance
heads bobbing   arms waving
faster and faster until
cast off puppets all
we fall to the floor   laughing
while the fading light
of the wishing star
caresses his face

The Changeling
(for my own Caliban-child)

What does it mean
to love a changeling child
fey goblin daughter   elfin son
the fairy child who chokes on earthly air
the moony-headed eyes that stare
the silent child who hears
a stranger's voice

idiot stumbler   shadow wraith
the child who crawls
like worm or snake   Caliban-child
with hoarded treasure   wild pixie
child who hates her mother
fish child with fins for arms and legs

the monster's mother   stoic-faced
spellbound sentry guards an ancient race
cradles the elf in the crook of her arm
the hopeful nurse   the witch's charm
our love the lock and key
to the wind-swept rooms of earth

where does the side-show child belong
what sad troll-mother chants
a nightmare song   what stranger calls
through deaf-mute dreaming
what wistful voices beckon   weeping
what far-off landscape longs
to take them home.

EDWARD L. HOOPER

I Know, You'd Rather Be Dead

Hallway whispers still echo
long after the pain was drugged off
and locked away in my mental stairwell.
I've heard your mezzanine words
fizz from my own mouth,
spilling out like warm numbing beer.
But death speaks a hot humid language
that forces the suck of air from a stone.

You see me happy and loved
like a birthday puppy,
yet you wonder
if it's a frothy mask;
mumming the screech of depression.
You must think me a fortress
to defend such a veil,
or see me more a carcass
hanging fish-dumb on some hook.

My muscles are atrophying,
and I gag on every bent walker
I ever swaggered by or thought to banter.
But Death?!

Do you imagine me gaily wheeling
into a square silk-lined box,
needing but two pallbearers?
Or do you know they'd lay me out
the same as you or your brother George—
Somehow dislocated from my round spoked legs?

The Way Downtown

on the sidewalk
         waiting
legs tingling
for the way downtown

it comes
like a giant windowed vacuum cleaner
sucking the corners of people
when it stops for me
i can't get on
         though
i've been faithful to trying

the driver unfolds the doors
and sees my wheels with the eyes of the pope
wanting to do more
    than a short prayer
        and speed off to his next stop

                                    but soon
             like a wounded elephant
             on its way to the secret burial-grounds
             the old hulk will lumber down to where
                       the crushed sedans
                       army tanks
                       rusty wheelchairs
                       and the rest all
                       snuggle together
             and it will lie down beside them

             so let the chevys and mitsubishis
             go gleaming by
                  as if i can drive a 5-speed
             i'll ride
                  yes
             i'll ride

III

NORMAN ANDREW KIRK

Crip

To bear the label of disabled is as dull
as any handicapped sameness of making wallets
for folding money or change which my hands
can't handle, so I prefer the word cripple
with the mythology of power and weakness
in the word, in the person of the word. But
"crip" is a word I promote by occasional
use, when there's a need for a noun for a name
beyond my name. The surface that others see.

Black Aggie

The whisper was recorded and rehearsed
from the red night districts of paper dust days
when the patients and professionals imagined
they saw the dirty writing men tattooed
on the secret surfaces of Black Aggie's skin.
She moved naked in my mind and dressed warmly
in my hand. Her crutches built perfect breasts
and dragged her rag-doll legs to whistling lust
for all the boys could know her since she'd go
to any dance. Ivory skin, black widow's hair,

Black Aggie had an hour for all, odors everywhere
of prehistoric mammals mating without care.
But her eyes! Stop the whispers. Give her black
aggie-eyes a chance to burn the grit into a tear.

The Tingle

My body fell asleep years ago. Cut off
at my neck by shattered bone fragments,
the line of my spine was bizarre. Alert,
my mind and soul prayed over my body's comas
for the burial of the dead, for the body's
resurrection. Spasms were electro-therapy
that increased its voltage as my muscles
twitched in an embryonic retreat to gain
again the lost dance of running grass anew.
Fire. My bed on fire! Quick, get a nurse!
"Is my bed on fire? Don, is my bed on fire?"
My skin was blazing. I tossed myself just
inches about with spasms, with arms a-fire,
flaying at imagined fires burning beneath me
burning through the mattress and rubber sheet,
burning the returning nerves into finite
disaster and no hope of repair. Time. Hurry.
Doctor help me. Doctor see me. Doctor. Doctor.

They came in answer to my pounding heart,
with white faces of care as we all feared
destruction beyond control. The sheets were
flung. The mattress shoved and bent. Ten arms
help me above the floor away from the fire.
I was saved. I felt saved. I felt love. All
of the faces of my friends began to smile.
Saved. We all loved our saving gift. All
having done all that there was to do. Fire?
Not a spark. Not a singe. No smoke. My spine
was a flaming tree within me with the flames
reaching my flesh, as I healed into wakefulness.
My body awakening in a flash from hell and
I lay burning in bed. All touch was flame but
I was a mystic lying on hot coals, not fearing
fires that eased into a tingle, the awakening
of sleeping hands. Today the slight tingle
of my body is a sensation few will know.
Unlike electric sparks, my skin does not dazzle
from the fire within and hands, all kinds of hands,
are like warm water, a kiss that takes fire's hot
melting into the warm glow of a natural comfort
as snug as body love, relaxed without release,
without the climactic claim of final conquest.
Hold me, if only in illusion. Feel the kicking stop.

ROBIN GATHANY SHEA

"Caught behind words..."

Caught behind words
Tangled webs of should and could
I am the child who cannot play
Imprisoned in the dictatorship
Of unprobed minds
Smiles and nods
That mask the fear
And

Teachers, who cannot learn
Save their conscience
With a dime
—For a quarter
I will cease to exist
Eliminate the pain
Of the store-front smile
And averted eyes

I'm the nonexistent being
The human error
The fatal flaw
I'll warp your world
With my ugliness
You cut me
With your pain.

"Don't smile . . ."

Don't smile
With puppy kindness
As I cross your path
Well-worn sidewalks
With sprawling cracks
I broke my mother's back
The mirror you hold
Before you smile
Shatters
In the glare of the sun
The fragments fall
Cutting my cheek
Tears of blood
Reflect
A thousand smiles

GLORIA MAXSON

Enid Field: In Memoriam

An agile voice, quick smile, and leaping eyes:
among the verities that bore her name,
and these things made one slow to realize,
quite incidentally, that she was lame.

The way she laughed if someone pitied her!
Calamity was just a kind of cloak
that one should wear akimbo, as it were,
with easy nonchalance—a kind of joke
was tragedy, that postured like a clown:
a trouble gone theatrical with age,
a grief got up in greasepaint, whose renown
depended on trick lighting and a stage.

Upheld by brace and crutch to common sight,
her grace was consummate, her footstep light.

Two Guitars

The Living
  As if in that far Pentecostal day,
    guitars were also filled with holy fire
    that gave the gift of tongues, you also may
    speak in whatever language you desire.

  It is not strange that woods so various
    as yours have moods as various as mine,
    that you can range from a gregarious
    flamenco shout or shrill electric whine
    that rocks the town, and then in full eclipse,
    begin a kind of lullabying croon
    that, with the tenderest of fingertips,
    can rock the cradle of the newborn moon.

  So speak in all your tongues, for all are true,
  and all are loved, for all of them are you.

The Dead
  How sad we sing no more in harmony,
    my old guitar, but both in silence lie!
    My fingers, stiffened with infirmity,
    no more evoke your strings to sweet reply,

    and my infirmity becomes your own
    in that shared sympathy that lovers know.

My broken voice has cracked the very tone
    of yours, that ranged so richly high and low,
    and the untimely bending of my form
    has set a subtle warping in your frame,
    as if you shared in every way the storm
    that came upon me, and that overcame.

So close were we in love, and joy, and art,
I tomb your silent body in my heart.

"Zotz!"

Zotz!!! You n*ame,it.kind of n.e.w. thing.EMERGing Merge of;blendING.///nOtIsOlated"""" boat ramps## 2 curbs.WE EXSIST.   mainly NATURE .gravity,,;towards existance fact(((—ON!WArds!!qoqaratonewa & yes.. whY NOT sum it all am are is ooowejebwe,sound of music   SPECIAL EFFECTS :it'sbility Stance WOW)))

Disabled Calligraphy

JOHN CROSSON

Cripple in Sight

Rigid in their dead man's stare,
The eyes have it.
Narrowed pupils dwell on my wrongs,
Overlook my rights,
Appraise my too human condition
As if they envision me
The personification of their own failures.

Now, under siege,
I have no recourse
But to retaliate likewise:
To weave my thoughts
Into two stubborn black blindfolds.
One for those eyes—
One for mine.

JANICE TOWNLEY MOORE

At the National Air and Space Museum

The silver Spirit of St. Louis
and the Wright Brothers' plane
hang luminously above

Blowing into a mouthpiece
he propels his unelectric limbs
through space   below

Near the Apollo spacecraft
moondust must fly like sparks
beneath his spinning wheels

moving right
left
right again

Aging he will not worry
about broken down parts
lean on a cane

His breath will carry him.

Reflections

Like an army of locusts
I hear a thin buzzing
that floats out of my chest
I am the crest of the shadow
the center cast upon mirrors
the mocking face

years have stained   have withered
images of a body   a feather blown
by odd winds of shine   of shade
images of a soul   the moon's hub unhinged
from the center rolls berserk

in the end everything runs out
runs under the wheels
a bandage unwinding
on the center line

when I most want the shadow
the infinite woman
who sleeps in my veins
to rise lightfooting
over long summer walks,
my ribs clang
like a metal signpost
at the edge of town

and the dark
I cannot shut out
crawls with me under the quilt:
I see all
moving to death
eyes in the mirror
glow dimmer than they were
drinking against me
thirstily

Suspension

It's all a blur of speed
the white wings
then nothing
but feeling numb
a trooper revolves overhead
a giant bug
ten arms   ten legs waving
before my face

I come to awareness
life reduced to the laws of gravity
and inertia   my mind suspended
my body the projector from another life
the time Mother caught me throwing paper
roll on roll into the bowl
"senseless" she said
and delivered her sermon on the sins
of waste   and I was convicted
wondering why I found it so exciting
the feel of paper through my hands
the sound of waterfalls
air passing beneath tires

I'm lifted up into the ambulance
carefully preserving my spine
that collapsible cup with all the wine
spilled out   all I know is the glare of headlights
the reflection from the back of my eyes
the moon   the stars collide
in a metaphor for my life   a white bird
pecking at black eyes
the vibrating red muscle
of my silent mouth

IV

NORMA THOMAS COLVIN

On Forgetting to Cry

Strange how
socks pulled over plastic toes
recall a wiggling delight severed years ago
And the shoes . . .
hideous with shine
can never know rock scars of being used . . .
    At least tomato seeds are sprouting
    on the back-porch
    demanding light and moisture
    only I can give
    powered by my wheelchair push
    to fill the watering-can and open blinds.

Cowboy-Boot Sale

Beyond
restless children littering popcorn
and hobblers trying out one boot
there
in a quiet corner
a wheelchair cages an immobile lady
Her husband lifts her stockinged foot
shoves on a boot
feels the fit and shifts the booted foot
back to the chair
The lady does not move or speak
        she can't
                But her blue eyes shine
                      like winning cowpokes' do

VIVIENNE FINCH

The Journey

There is a long journey to be made:
across a room

travellers tell of the vast dimensions
of the pyramids and other great ruins,
but utterly insignificant are the greatest of these
when compared to the mountain of this stone,

that structure an interaction of energies

and the deeper urgency of love confusions,
the vital experience of *meeting* a stare;

all that to think of, but
"nothing will matter
if only you are ready for it"

and as a single tree I look to become solid,
a numen of the woods
searching out a healing

as the whiteness of a body shines
so do the dark wounds glisten,

movements that are disturbances of light
components bringing unity to disfigurement,
the edge of things glowing

and because of what happened/is happening *here*
this place becomes the most important there is:

I need to stay, hold to familiarity—
what is *known* is loved
for we met such truth in closeness

and are learning to forget distances,
the impulsive song: "soon it will end,
true singing is a different kind of breath,
a breath about nothing, a wind"

the morning calm is misleading,
its deadness offering a kind of luminosity
that gazes through paper,
challenges the room-span
its blankness

and how it ends.

On Being Stone

what it is to be stone
where the texture of pain is unique

to shrink from sudden glare
though stars remain alert

to wince when forces fail
when the cordite erupts
through seams of granite flank

to be stone
that is always an obstacle
with nothing to contravene
the blackness of its core

that can only watch
the coital fluttering of shadow
moon turning a blind eye
to the huge figure of sleep
sublimated by abstracts

to glow white
even in darkness
a pantheon of mysteries
inflamed by axe-hewn scars

to be stone
invoking arctic anaesthesia

to sorrow like a secret door
that is rolled aside
for the second coming

waiting to meet more stone

but in meeting find no face
in parting follow no retreat
in speaking
make no sound
being no being

longing to be the rose
to own a body
wherein everything happens
where all variations of colour
are possible

and being that rose
recuperate from being born
just to find
it was a mistake

but that being stone
find no tears are allowed
for they simply turn to pebbles

to the beginning of being stone

An Earthquake Somewhere Else
(which has something to do with loneliness)

Darkly in vesper stillness
comes the wavering scream of trains

And somewhere
in the marrow of distance,
the earth's crust is
               disturbed

shocked into fracture

convolute as coral,
convulsing like my brain

Simultaneous actualities,
subject
to the same great stress,

where rock and brain are
               blemished
where both admit the flaw

and are almost moonstruck
by the knowledge
          of that weakness

We shear and dislocate
across the bulk of earth,
             propagated
by the same nucleus
the same vibrating fibres
same trembling cytoplasms

overpowered
by linear acceleration
attacked
by similar cobalt rays,

where uncertainty
has something to do with loneliness
the steady centre
           collapses

and the crucible shatters
into stagnant shards,
spilling the waters
         culled
from stone and sorrel source

And the echo pains
      as it deepens
spinestiff to midnight

II
I am dressed in white;
the sky of a strange room
lowers a cloud into my mouth
where it swells like a sponge,

and one cough
from a tesselated throat
is a relic of breathing
that ignites
into the purple glare of amnesia,
as a corner of the nightmare
recedes
beyond the angle of parallax.

Dressed in white,
while an offering of fruit
blackens
on the table,

(and there is a scent of green apples,
but only if you concentrate),

mindsketching what is left over,
the shadows, petals, spilt water,
stains like barrelled woodlice,

belonging somewhere else
but not sure where,

passing through the dividable sea,
dispersed,
collected together
and again dispersed,

finding what is left
is fragile,
brimful of fear,
and like progress
infected with acute stasis,

suspended
like an incomplete sentence,

and this pain is like a person
for whom indulgence is asked,

like an earthquake
landsliding to sensory nerveblock.

We are windhewn detritus
of brain and rock,
the stony flesh of earth,

still surviving.

III
skin is cooled
        with volatile liquids

think cold

water cramps bone
        walking will be awkward
in this pack of ice,

fingers seem further away
than a mere armslength,

doorways darkclose;

think cold
lose contact
but fight

for a corpse
is happening to the earth,
mutating slow
        and wormwhite
as that vulnerable grating
of weak skin in the skull
        is broken open;

already the room is curtained off
by the clatter of surgical hatching

this is absolute isolation

so transparently impenetrable,
and something to do with loneliness;

do not move
think cold
lose contact

go to the island of wild olives,
beyond the silver disc of pain,
and the olives sliced by sun
        will heal
        will erase the stigmata
like Easter when the sun dances;

but for now flesh sweats,
smells old,
blood flows
slow as molasses,

yet has potential.

IV
I exist through simultaneous events,
from areas of science
to mythology,

unable to separate
the too dense fabric
of voices.

The eagle has sharpened his beak
and enters rock
by a bloodless gash,

and his wingblade
spills rhythmic adrenalin
from that cranial split;

like talon on rock,
all breathing claws at the surface,
and an annular groove,
a scission in the skull,
bares white association fibres.

Probe
dovetails
lobes and thalamus

know this
they say

all is towards an ending
becoming a beginning.

Intense and luminous,
the leucotome of hot gold wire
thrusts seizmic jolts
into the book of storms,

cold the sweat runs down,
convulse, contort,
the grey and white—
the flame is blue
the fire is ice;

yet it burns
and seals my lips

take out my tongue
for I am guilty
of stealing your words

destroy my moving
for I am guilty
of abandoning you

but do not let your blade slip,
the blade forceful even in shadow,

with its own law,
its personal lyric
carving ugly vowels,

do not make me other than I am

help me yet from this white hot heat
that hawkwing cannot penetrate,

shed tears
so I may drown
for I was christened by the sound
of my own screaming.

No candle flames at my feet,
and all images are severed,
refracted in a vortex of water;

but this swelling is benign,
do not invade these hemispheres again,

for the night has no more healing.

v
and the dream eagle scavenges
        a zodiac
           for the strength
to replenish its legend

its beakprobe drags
an anvil of deep amber
        from the sun's eclipse
to feed its rocknest
with raw energy

water is cracking around me
        like parchment
the bones of the mountain
        are settling

red berries of dogweed
have not swollen
            escape the eagle
but their flame spirals
            through my eyes
to break across wounded bone
            like a moon in seizure

the incursion over
            I am waking abruptly
to incisions still secret to the eye
wounds that are swabbed by clouds
            as cold as frost fire
and snow rising from earth
like a white wound bleeding
            the chromosomes divide
create the impossible alliance
            of panic and serenity

last rays destroy
            eradicate
until images are primitively clear
            and a weary arm
hangs like the limb
of David's dead Marat

and there is a scent of green apples
(but only if you concentrate)

VI

birdsong winds down to a stammer
sky empties
and tilts into the room
at crazy angles

still dressed in white

with a flame
licking gently
along lashes

only the throats of tulips
are annealed by the retreat of echoes
thinking that they exist
that memory is true to its colour

the night has found a little healing

though the room is tongueless
quiet and tight as root

now only ice cuts the nacre of flesh
and is something to do with loneliness

but along the rubble of the faultline
the coral flowers
have almost bloomed to death

again the augury of blossom fails

DEBORAH KENDRICK

For Mama

Mama never rocked me.
No cuddling close to crumble terrors,
No lullabies for lonely hours,
No flesh-on-flesh confusion.

Oh, once perhaps . . .
Home from hospital . . .
Still learning to be a blind child,
Quarreling with my brother for a toy,
I had fallen down cellarstairs backward.
All scrunched up close and rocking,
She cradled me with tension.
She was seeking her own solace—not mine,
And she set me free, exhausted.
And it was only once.

Now I shudder from her embraces.
The annual empty hug.
Her whisky eats her memories,
Sparsely dotted by my childhood:
An erasure of ineffable pain.

So, now . . . trying to find that littler me,
I rock my babies tenderly.
Comforted vicariously,
I ache to feel their joy.

A Question of Art

Like something very precious, he holds it in his hands.
He has fashioned such art himself and so he knows
to touch only the corners, not to let so much as
one finger brush its glossy black-and-white perfection.
Almost reverently, he holds this thick rectangle of
paper and says, "It captures you. It is the essence
of the woman I have fallen in love with."
His gladness at the thing is contagious.
It wraps me warm, seduces me, fills me up more full
than a sexual rush of recognition.

I want to share in this five-by-seven bit of sorcery,
and I want to know why it is so rare.
Is it a magic trick performed by California sunlight?
Or the emergence of some light inside myself
that surfaced just as the artist pressed the button?
Was the wholeness of being so loved and in love
mingled with just the right shaft of light to create this
    miraculous thing?

I want to make him smile like this forever.
I want to assimilate these elusive qualities he is
holding there, preserve for him this joy, keep him so kind.
I want to learn to arrange my face just so—
like tying a scarf at just the right angle.

But he can not translate them for me into words.
And I have never seen this "essence" in a mirror.
I have never looked at this photograph
or any other. . . .
I have never seen his face . . .
or mine.
And, I am so afraid that what he loves
is locked up in this two-dimensional image, and
that he will never hold the real me with such tenderness.

Me and Hercule Poirot

People always tell me things—
intimate pieces of insanity.
Secret confessions, paranoid regressions,
electives and perspectives—I've heard them all.

Little old ladies go to great lengths
to sit beside me on buses.
They look earnestly into my face and
immediately air ancient grievances.
Their voices warble, skittering up and down
like beautiful birds' songs
and they smell of lavender and wheat toast.
I learn about bursitis, colitis, arthritis,
letters written by dead husbands,
negligent or doting children,

and the idiosyncrasies of dying cronies from the nursing home.
With meticulous detail they reveal to me
the process and contents for building perfect biscuits and pies.

Younger women crowd into rows with me at seminars.
They laugh hollowly of hysterectomies, post-partum hemorrhoids,
and other personal injustices:
affairs with married men, lesbian tendencies,
assorted yearnings for attention—
I hear about them all.

Old men bring me flowers.
Some reek of cheap wine and decaying garments;
I remind them of some daughter who probably never existed.
The more polished ones lament
smashed poetry careers,
youthful prison terms,
or just more love gone awry.

Flabby teenaged boys whisper conspiratorially
of hearts they wish they'd broken,
books they haven't the sense to read,
. . . pathetic imagined adventures.
The burgers they push into their faces
splash unfortunately as they whine
and I, the victim, absorb every syllable.

Pretty people tell me things, too.
Gala affairs with inadequate crepes,
the trauma of losing the maid,
or a long-suppressed morsel of bigotry.
I am easy to talk to they all say.
I'm not sure why I'm always selected.
They sense a foreign otherness, I suppose,
think me not entirely one of them . . .
I know my little gray cells are certainly invisible—
though it may be my fancy mustaches.

LAURIE STROBLAS

How to Sign

Invent and *father* are said at the forehead.
Mother comes out from the chin.
On the bumpy nose sits *fool*.
You won't learn the sign for yes until page 112.
No is a beak prattling to its shadow.
In front of the mouth scratches *bird*.
Squeeze the bird once or twice in your hand
to get *orange*. Now you can do anything.
Teach your fingers to spell without you.
Make an island, start a river.
Build a floodgate and walk the width
to let it know your weight.
Test the water with your toes.
Now you can say almost anything.
The line for the past moves back
over the right shoulder.
Stop flailing your arms.
When you finally learn *yes*
it will be a fist knocking.

FREDERICA GOLDSMITH

Capes

They swathed me in
cascading capes
hiding the hurt—
lest I be horrendous
to behold—
while Polish children
silently snickered,
"*Garbus! Garbus!*"*

A child—I romped like the rest
as the mini-mantle
billowed behind.
Classmates pulled and plucked
the concealing cloak
silently snickering,
"*Garbus! Garbus!*"

Time passed. I migrated to
distant lands and
shed the screening shroud
fleeing from torments.
Yet—at this late date,
at the sight of a cape,
I hear a
silent snicker,
"*Garbus! Garbus!*"

*"*Hunchback!*"

EVELYN THOMAS

Covering All Bases

Lazarus-like, I am restored
Thank you god, thank you mrs. god,
Thank you infinite void,
Thank you existential absurd,
Thank you
For letting me live.

JACK HAND

Pain Is My Brother

Pain is my brother,
My most constant friend. . . .
I am a beached whale,
Gasping out my last hours
On the shore of the Great South Bay,
A diversion for children
Who stone me and prod my sides
With driftwood spears
Until I am eager to be dogfood
Or garbage.
I am a stunned shark
In the shallows at Pass de Grilles,
Bludgeoned by tourists from Akron,
Blood blinding my eyes,
My teeth soon to dangle
From keychains at Rotary breakfasts.
Alive now only in pain,
I am the spider held by my own thread
Over the fire,
The frog stuffed with a firecracker
On the Fourth of July,
The mustang whose lungs
Have burst to bloody froth
Under the lazy spiral
Of the helicopter,

Who stumbles and welcomes
The brain-shattering bullet.
Pain is my brother,
My most constant friend. . . .
Death is what
I know of God.

Death Stairs/Life House

My bootheels and my cane
Stick in the drillholes
Where they blasted out
These seven hundred pound
Granite blocks that
Step up the hill to your house.
I am alone as dusk gathers,
Thinking about what you told me
As the pain floods and ebbs
Around my hips and spine.
How you and your wife
Rediscovered the lever
And roller, strained
To topple each slab
Onto your lowbed trailer.
A labor worth it, you said,
To switch back this steep hill
With immortal granite stairs,

Laying each block in
So the legends were covered,
Each misspelled name or wrong date,
Each simple slab traded up
By money-proud children.
You wondered how the dead
Would feel, having chosen
Their own honest granite,
To lie now beneath
Two thousand pounds of simpering angels.
You got them cheap. Labor costs
Too much to cut off and recarve.
No one would admit to wanting
A monument used before,
And who could be sure
Whose used death
They were buying?
The pain ebbs.
At the top of the hill
You are waiting with a glass
Of last year's scuppernong wine.
We will sit on the steps
Of the house you built yourselves,
Every stick and stone.
As dark comes slowly on
We will make a circuit
Around this house,
Your homeplace now
In a way few ever know,
Inspect the garden,

Look over the trees
At your neighbor's Catawba vineyard,
The last red of the Carolina sun
Bringing down stark darkness.
We will gather for a while
Before your fieldstone hearth
Before I make that
Long journey down
The death stairs,
Drill holes catching
Again at my heels, my cane,
Those impassive blocks of granite,
Which tell their messages silently
To the earth, reminding me
Where I, too, am headed.

Pain
(For D.N.)

These two, dissimilar, understood—
Pope and Byron—
How the eye thickens like a Mongol's face,
And the attention wanders
In the slow drone of the body's scream.
They knew these nights without sleep,
The fire nesting in each nerve's end,
And these mornings, stiff with fatigue,
When the spine is sharp, and the body
Cold in the sun's heat.
They knew this life:
This dance on the cerebrum, these bootheels
On the heart.

V

ZANA

broken

i don't cry because it was my favorite glass
but squat here on the floor, tears forming
because it is all so hard
these days.
to arrange
my body down here
this low.   to lift
the splinters and the arcs
in dustpan, to transport them
to a safer place.
unexpected major chore
in the scheme of a day.
most of all i cry
for the ice cubes
dusty, melting on the floor
for i craved cold water
and they were
all i had.

A Question of Energy

I'm not diminished
    by this loss of limb
I'm more than
    the sum of my parts
to deny my scars
    is to deny my power
the core of heat in each cell.

I've got wires humming
    juice surging
        detours on the path
it takes less time now
less resistance
to complete the circuit.

        I'm well grounded
            you can touch me
                without a shock.

Mirage
    for Les Breese

The accident
that took my leg
took
your life.

Now you approach
again and again
    ghost rider
        tracking my dreams.
Hooves gallop
    across molten lavabeds
Pound a chant
    in the dust of red clay
Pound a trail
    around my parched flesh.
You vanish
    into the shimmer of canyon echoes
Desire
    thunders in your wake.

Questions

1.

They stare:
a woman about my age
her young son in the shopping cart.
I maneuver down the aisle on crutches
she averts her eyes.
He smiles   I smile back.
"Where is your leg? What happened to your leg?"
Before I can respond she slaps him hard
shoves the cart ahead.
He sobs   looks back in horror
the questions thistle in his throat.
"Wait!"
She turns the corner.
I swallow my answers
choke on their bitter roots.

2.

Boldly smirking
he watches me move
from washing machine to dryer
approaches   cracking his gum
"Why ya limping?
Artificial leg, huh?
Yeah, I thought so.
I had a woman once with one leg,

she took better care of me than most with two."
He blocks my way.
"Maybe you'd like to take care of me for awhile?"

3.
She staggers from the bar to our table
clutches my arm
her coal black hair   painted face
too close to mine.
"Such a pretty girl.
If that happened to me I'd kill myself."
I look at her, this woman
old enough to be my mother.
"Why, why would you do that?"
"It's tough enough being a woman," she says.

4.
On our wedding day
my father-in-law asks,
"Why couldn't you have picked someone
with all of her parts?"

MICHAEL CLEARY

Fingers, Fists, Gabriel's Wings

My voice, plucked from the air,
clasped in the interpreter's hands:
fists bloom, close,
pulse of hothouse flowers;
supple fingerpuppet dancers
move to unsounded strains.

Watching the deaf girl listen,
I think there is more to words
than sound ever knows,
brimming handfuls of speech
tempered by secondhand grace.
The word, unutterably, made flesh:
fingers flutter, hover, fold,
the whisk of Gabriel's wings.

H. N. BECKERMAN

"To: The Access Committee . . ."

"To:
 The Access Committee,
Attention:
 Handicapped Romeo.
  There is now a suitable ramp
 installed at my balcony.
  Impatiently,
   Miss Juliet

Adjustments

I know you'd do anything for me,
wheeled lover.
So why did you leave
the cupboard door open,
the point gouging my forehead
and once my eye?
Oh, only those?
As for me, I'll try harder
to remember, too.
As for you,
you'll just have to watch
where you go!
More, precious?
Don't be angry;
Braille me the whole list!

WILLIAM D. CRAGO

". . . where late the sweet birds sang"

I could say that
Gestapo troops of cancer
Blitzkrieged my spine,
Beheading me, so to speak,
Leaving me for dead—neck down.
So, now, this temple
(so I've heard it called)
Holds communion only in the balcony.
Should I go on
To speak metaphorically
Of the church below,
That ruined altar
No priest will ever serve?
I've heard of boys
Cut short
To keep their voices sweet—
Knife instead of wife
You might say,
To help them sing;
But this castration
Quiets my choir,
Stuns my spring.

Subterfuge

I remember my father, slight,
staggering in with his Underwood,
bearing it in his arms like an awkward bouquet

for his spastic child who sits down
on the floor, one knee on the frame
of the typewriter, and holding her left wrist

with her right hand, in that precision known
to the crippled, pecks at the keys
with a sparrow's preoccupation.

Falling by chance on rhyme, novel and curious bubble
blown with a magic pipe, she tries them over and over,
spellbound by life's clashing in accord or against itself,

pretending pretense and playing at playing,
she does her childhood backward as children do,
her fun a delaying action against what she knows.

My father must lose her, his runaway on her treadmill,
will lose the terrible favor that life has done him
as she toils at tomorrow, tensed at her makeshift toy.

Spastic Child

A silk of flame composed his hair to fleck
His cheeks with freckles dappled on his pallor,
Misplaced like cartoons on a pall, to spatter
His chin laced with a silver thread of spittle
His wax doll hands cannot wipe off. Subsuming
The muted tragedies of moth and mote
Like crucifixes wrought in ivory,
His tongue, slight mollusk broken in its shell,
Is locked so minnows of his wit may never
Leap playing in our waterspouts of words
For the sheer luxury of diving back
Into the pools of quietude, inlaid
With leaves the autumn-umber of his eyes—
His mind, bright bird, forever trapped in silence.

Sampson

Sampson sulking in jail regretted his
eyes and Delilah—especially, though,
his hair (not that he was sissy or
crazy, in fact, just the opposite of
either), but he lamented his strength which
for some wild reason had been in those

curls of his, which had driven Delilah
wild—was she a hair-freak or what, he would
wonder when she would finger his hair till he grew
wild himself—but now he knew so well what
she'd wanted had been the dark snarl of his
strength all along ravelled over her cream
skin, and while he remembered, his guards kept
taunting, "Don't cry, they'll grow back, your
locks, your eyes too maybe." Sampson roared, "God
damn! it isn't my hair or my eyes, it's
my strength, it's my life, the jawbone of
the ass I killed some of you Philistines
with, that lion I choked with these bare
hands, eating the honey right out of his
carcass, good to my tongue . . ." "Oh, all
right," sighed one old gray-haired guard. "You're getting
    riled
up again, and do you have to cuss quite so
much; every one's in trouble enough as
it is, even us!" "Much the likes of you'd
know!" Sampson answered him back. "Besides.
I don't cuss. Moses says 'Thou shalt not take the
name of the Lord in vain,' and me, when I take it, by
God, I mean it!" "All right, you
win!" The keeper was tired. "The older I
get, the less I know whether I swear or
pray to my gods!" "Both of you, butt out!" bellowed
some one, "and, Sampson, admit it, you
just can't handle life now!" "Give me a million
years more and I might," the big man yelled, and

suddenly leaped tall to his grief, stretched toward
his anger, planting himself between two
posts, wrapped an arm around each, and howled, "It
is death I can't handle, not life" till leaning
hard forward with muttering prayer, he
merged into ruins—and he handled it.

Dramatic Monologue in the Speaker's Own Voice

I walk naked under my clothes like anyone else,
and I'm not a bomb to explode in your hands.
Of course, you are not (I would not accuse you of)
thinking of holding me down, but of holding me up.
Yet sometimes I'd love to be eased from the envelope of
    sleep,
stroked gently open (although it would take some
    doing—
on my part, that is). My lost virginity
would hurt me the way the ghosts of their limbs
make amputees shriek, my womanhood
too seldom used. Have you ever viewed me this way?
No, none of you ever have. I'm either a monster
in search of a horror movie to be in,
or else I'm a brain floating within a body
whose sides I must gingerly touch while you glance

discreetly away. Sometimes when you hear it go—bump!
it gives you a nasty shock after which you insist I am
 glued
to my flesh like a fly in a paste pot. Maybe you think
 everyone is,
that, or a delicate lady in a dirty sty mincing on tiptoe.
I wish you'd learn better before we all totter
into our coffins where there's no straight way to lie
 crooked.

FELIX POLLAK

Reality

The streets are full of people moving
in thickets of snowfall—animated marionettes,
the reel of a silent flick strewn with dead white
moths. Their voices are drowned out by the tinkling
of an ancient piano in the pit, played by an old man
with numb fingers. Overhead, hidden by the tight mesh,
the tinkling of tinsel, thin icicles breaking.

My eyes reach out
but cannot touch. It is like
trying to feel with frozen fingers,
it is like numbness being touched.
The reality of things is hidden
behind a spiderweb
that gives but will not yield.
There are no entrances, no exits.
The outside world will forever remain
just that. Everyone, everything is
saying, *Noli me tangere*.

My eyes remember
the forgetting of sight.

They remember the melting
of contours, the fading away
of colors. My eyes have memories
of losses. My eyes are forgetting
to remember.

It is like speech going
into silence—into
muteness. It is a deafening
of eyes, it is like a candle's
burning past its wick, it is
like impotence, as one lies
beside the beloved.

———

Intolerables
are a succession of stairs:
one intolerable
always leading to another.

———

I dreamed I picked up
a blind man's white cane
by mistake, then could not
find the place to return it.

Tunnel Visions

I.

First the light cracked
and black hairlines appeared.
Then tiny pores opened like peepholes,
for the night to peer in,
the winds of the void to blow through.
Crumbs of grey started to drown,
floating downward, out of sight,
islands sinking in a tide.
Colors slid into shafts of blindspots,
the memories of shapes sailed the seven
black seas.

II.

Her voice enters the room,
followed by her form and only last
her face, a flower, a small cloud
of smoke. I knew this face when it was
white, distinct, bordered by black hair.
Now the hair, too, has wilted,
turned grey.

III.

I wake to the sound of rain.
Scent of wet grass. It is
still night. The world is all right

at this hour. There is nothing
to look at. A bird begins to proclaim
his ownership of our tree. Over and
over. No dispute.
Soon dawn will invade my window,
crawl up to my door. Peace is
running out. Not peace: armistice.
I close my eyes, sink back into
my dream. My eyes are opened,
become as clear and sharp
as a bird's.

IV.
Another transparent skin has grown
over the world since I last met it.
I am descending the black keys
of a piano. They sing
>   *Keep well*
>   *Keep safe*
>   *Keep*

Some of the white keys counter with
>   *But*
>   *Yet*
>   *Still*

Gradually, though, the piano falls silent,
like letters from estranged friends,
like dusk falling over a street corner,
creating a dead end. Slowly,
the world contracts, wrapped
in a musty smell.

Tunnel Visions

I.
First the light cracked
and black hairlines appeared.
Then tiny pores opened like peepholes,
for the night to peer in,
the winds of the void to blow through.
Crumbs of grey started to drown,
floating downward, out of sight,
islands sinking in a tide.
Colors slid into shafts of blindspots,
the memories of shapes sailed the seven
black seas.

II.
Her voice enters the room,
followed by her form and only last
her face, a flower, a small cloud
of smoke. I knew this face when it was
white, distinct, bordered by black hair.
Now the hair, too, has wilted,
turned grey.

III.
I wake to the sound of rain.
Scent of wet grass. It is
still night. The world is all right

at this hour. There is nothing
to look at. A bird begins to proclaim
his ownership of our tree. Over and
over. No dispute.
Soon dawn will invade my window,
crawl up to my door. Peace is
running out. Not peace: armistice.
I close my eyes, sink back into
my dream. My eyes are opened,
become as clear and sharp
as a bird's.

.

IV.

Another transparent skin has grown
over the world since I last met it.
I am descending the black keys
of a piano. They sing
> *Keep well*
> *Keep safe*
> *Keep*

Some of the white keys counter with
> *But*
> *Yet*
> *Still*

Gradually, though, the piano falls silent,
like letters from estranged friends,
like dusk falling over a street corner,
creating a dead end. Slowly,
the world contracts, wrapped
in a musty smell.

The Finger

The foreign land has not become home,
but home a foreign land.
—Alfred Polgar

I.
I look out of my window at night
in Madison, Wisconsin,
and am in the midst of London's crime,
small shrouds suffocating the gaslights,
Jack the Ripper stalking his prey.

I pull the curtain and turn out the light.
Night joins me to all who are well.
In the dark now, like me, they see
no-sights as I. They and I become
a black-on-black canvas in the Museum
of Modern Art.

II.
I dream of the finger of the statue
on top of the Burgtheater in Vienna.
From it flew, a life ago, a bird,
into a blue hole in the sky. I followed him
high up with my eyes, my eyes became winged
by the bird, it was an epiphany of joy.

In all my exiled years of home
within no home, that marble finger,
that long dead bird, were my secret
homeland, re-enacted in flashes and
dreams. I saw the bird alight again,
a symbol of escape, when my First Papers
were stamped with FRIENDLY ALIEN. I have
remained so, all these years.

I have been back. I've pilgrimaged to that vision,
that unchanged finger pointing upwards past
Buchenwald and Dachau, past a war, past
the evaporation of once-upon-a-time. I've never
told my secret. But I was home again,
a boy again, for moments.

III.
I may pass through once more next month.
But it will not be Vienna. It will be
London's fog. I will not see that finger,
nor that statue. If I am lucky,
I'll go to my hotel one night
and have a dream.

Incident

The bank foyer is plush. People pass
through pulsating gauze curtains and black
mirrors, glittering with sundrops. Dazzled,
I stop at one of the desks and ask for the use
of a phone. "Right over there, Sir," a pleasant
girlish voice says, "at the second desk."
I touch white and dark shiny objects, a plant,
the keys of an adding machine, the frame of
what must be a desk calendar. I hear a suppressed
giggle and the girlish voice whispering, "Hey, Bob
—look at that!" I brace myself, my hand sliding
across the desk. "Warm . . . no, cold . . . the *white*
one . . . *hot* . . . there you go!" My finger slips off
the push buttons. A male voice at my side says,
"Dial 9 for outside, Sir. May I help you?"

When we played *Blinde Kuh* in the park, blindfolded,
dizzily spun around, groping for arms, backs, bellies,
still too innocent to try for a budding breast, but
already strangely enticed by the different smell of
long hair, tottering, clumsily clowning and
laughing out of breath, it was fun without fright.
We tore off our handkerchiefs, the world instantly
in place, our balance restored, as we eye-gagged our
victim and teased him into a lamp post.

The hush cold on my skin, I stride towards the exit,
through glittering gauze and lightshafts sharp as
knives, pretending swiftness and sureness as I steer
into the rectangular frame of light and feel the door give
as I push. Air! Noise! The street!

How I used to hate emerging out of the long tunnels
on the train that took us to Marienbad every summer,
to grandparents and the two goats I loved. I was
too proud to hold on to my mother's hand as I sat in the
delicious darkness filled with anything-can-happen,
the blood-curdling cry, the sound of a passionate kiss,
the suicide of the lean black man in the corner
who looked like a spy—O how I hated the flickers
of daylight returning through the windows and the
    triumphant
whistle crying, *We've made it!, we're back to normal,
now everything will be safe again, and dull*!

I stand on the street, and there's no time to lose,
this is the moment to join the group that is crossing
the street. Wherefrom the sudden insane thought,
as I wait for the bus: *Is the skin of my face growing
over my eyes?* I resist the impulse to look into
the mirror of a store window. I know there would be
no reply.

Biographical Sketches of the Contributors

JOHN MANN ASTRACHAN was born in 1928 in New York City, where he is currently a physician and practicing psychiatrist. He is also Associate Clinical Professor of Psychiatry in Obstetrics and Gynecology at the New York Hospital–Cornell Medical Center. He began writing poetry in 1978, and since then has published his poetry in both medical and literary journals, including *The New England Journal of Medicine*, *Journal of the American Medical Association*, and *Negative Capabilities*.

MICHAEL BACHSTEIN was born in 1955 in Decatur, Illinois, and has attended Southern Illinois University at Carbondale and the University of Louisville. His poems have appeared in several literary journals, including *Nimrod*, *Hiram Poetry Review*, and *In a Nutshell*. In addition to writing poetry, he is currently at work on a novel.

H. N. BECKERMAN was born on Thanksgiving Day, 1913, in Greenwich Village, New York. A retired photographer, Beckerman enjoys reading widely, enabling him, in his words, to "solve modern problems." He is also active in the art world and has recently displayed "a construction on bio-ethics," entitled "New Answers, New Questions at Age 69," at a New York Bank. His publications encompass a variety of subjects, including an article on electromagnetic shaping systems to be published in a forthcoming issue of *Beruf* magazine. His poetry has appeared in several journals, most recently in *Potpourri*, a publication of St. Margaret's House, a New York home for disabled residents.

HAROLD BOND was born in Boston to first-generation parents of Armenian ancestry, and presently lives in Melrose, Massachusetts. He received his A.B. in English-journalism from Northeastern University and his M.F.A. in creative writing from the University of Iowa. Currently a creative writing teacher at the Cambridge Center for Adult Education, he has also worked extensively as visiting poet-in-the-schools in Massachusetts and other New England states. In 1976, he was the recipient of a creative writing fellowship grant from the National Endowment for the Arts. He has published three volumes of poetry, and his most recent work, *The Way It Happens to You*, was published in 1979. His poems have appeared widely in magazines, including *The New Yorker*, *Harper's Magazine*, *Saturday Review*, and *The New Republic*, as well as in numerous anthologies of contemporary American writing.

MICHAEL CLEARY was born in Schenectady, New York, in 1945. Since receiving his Ph.D., he has taught English and creative writing classes at Broward Community College in Ft. Lauderdale, Florida. He has published numerous poems and essays in critical anthologies and literary journals, including recent issues of *The Appalachee Quarterly*, *The Seattle Review*, *Gryphon*, *The Texas Review*, and *Anthology of Magazine Verse and Yearbook of American Poetry*.

NORMA THOMAS COLVIN, daughter of pioneer parents, spent her childhood in the mountain wilderness of copper mines and the deserts of Arizona. Preparing for a career in commercial art and advertising, she studied at the Phoenix Junior College, the Art Center in Los Angeles, the University of Alaska, and the Museum Art School in Portland, Oregon. She has exhibited work in the fine arts in numerous galleries and juried shows in Alaska and the state of Washington. From her interest in establishing rapport between communities and their artists, she has founded several art leagues and gallery groups in the eastern Washington area. Her poetry has been published widely in numerous journals and anthologies, including *Pen Woman*, *Harpoon*, *The Pittsburgh Press Anthology*, and *The Olympian*.

WILLIAM D. CRAGO, a native of Detroit, Michigan, is currently Associate Professor of English at Kentucky Wesleyan College, with his area of teaching emphasis in nineteenth-century American literature. He lives with his wife and two children in Owensboro, Kentucky. In addition to teaching and writing, he enjoys gardening, carpentry, and playing ragtime piano. Crago, former editor of the *Green River Review*, first began publishing his poetry in 1984. Since then, his poems have appeared in several literary journals, including *Piedmont Literary Review* and *Tempest* and in the anthology *Men Talk*.

JOHN CROSSON was born in 1943 in Camden, New Jersey. He is currently a resident of the state of California, where he is at work on a collection of short stories.

MARILYN DAVIS was born in New Haven, Connecticut, in 1949 and has lived in northeastern Ohio nearly all her life. She is currently writing a dissertation on the novels of George Eliot to complete the Ph.D. requirements in English at Kent State University, where she is also a teaching fellow. She published a chapbook of poems, called *Twenty-Eight Days*, in 1981 and often reads her work at area poetry readings. Her son, Cody, was born in 1973.

NEDINE DAVIS lives in Tacoma, Washington, with her husband and their two children. In 1953, she received her B.A. from Eastern Washington University. Since college, she has served as Assistant to the Dean of Women at Western Montana College, and, more recently, she has done extensive work with the United Way of Spokane. She traces the beginning of her writing career to her days as a journalist for her high school and college newspapers. Her poetry has been published in numerous national and international literary journals, including *Kaleidoscope* and *You 'n Me*. In addition, her poetry has appeared widely in local newspapers and journals of the Northwest, where she is active in several writer's clubs.

SUSAN L. DUNN was born in 1947 in Washington, D.C. Until her death in 1982, she had a special love of horses and considerable skill as an equestrian. In 1969, she earned a degree in elementary education with a minor in theater from the University of Maryland. In the same year, she experienced a fall from a horse that, together with her diabetes, resulted in the loss of her sight. She resumed riding in 1974 and began a therapeutic horseback-riding program for children from the Maryland School for the Blind. A talented public speaker on the effects of blindness and diabetes, she was also well known for her theatrical accomplishments, both as a performer and a writer. In 1980, she completed her first play, *The Drummer I Must March To?*, which was produced at the University of Maryland and subsequently broadcast by National Public Radio as a one-hour special. At various times, she acted the leading role in the play and assisted in its production.

VIVIENNE FINCH, a resident of the United Kingdom, is a freelance journalist and translator, whose work includes reviewing for the *Times Literary Supplement*. She has performed in London's West End poetry, dance, and theater groups; has broadcast poetry, both her own and others', for the BBC; and has founded her own press, Tangent Books. She presently serves as fund-raiser for SEQUAL and as editor of *Possibility*, a journal sponsored by the same organization. Her poetry has been published in numerous literary journals and often anthologized, most recently in the *Virago Book of Women Poets*. She has also published several volumes of poetry, including *Interactions*, a poetry novel.

S. L. FRIEDMAN was born in 1908 in Philadelphia, Pennsylvania, and has lived in the Los Angeles area since 1941. A retired business manager in a commercial field, Friedman has a special interest in the arts, and reports having occasionally taken a day off work to "nurture a nascent poem." He has published *The Glass Shore*, a chapbook of poetry.

MARY R. GAUMOND is a native of Waterford, New York, and currently lives in Bowie, Maryland, with Paul, her husband. Since the early 1970's, when she won first prize in a local poetry contest and began writing in earnest, she has been the recipient of various awards for poetry and prose. In addition to serving as coordinator of the Beta Poetry Workshop, she is currently a member of the Maryland State Poetry Society and the National League of American Pen Women. Her poems have appeared in many literary journals and anthologies, including *The American Poetry League Magazine, Pteranodon, Hephaestus*, and *Rye Bread: Women Poets Rising*. She is presently studying typesetting in preparation for the publication of a collection of poems on a home press.

JAN GLADING, whose parents lived in Mexico, was born just north of the border in El Paso, Texas, because her parents wished to ensure her United States citizenship. Her youth was spent in California, where she returned with her husband and four children after spending several years in Texas and New York. She received her B.A. in language arts in 1958 from the University of California at Berkeley, and taught literature and composition to high school students, until the onset of osteoarthritis led to her early retirement in 1969. In 1975 at age fifty-one, she received her M.A. in creative writing from San Francisco State University. She has twice been a fellow at Squaw Valley and has attended several poetry conferences at Foothill College and Napa Valley College in California.

FREDERICA GOLDSMITH was born in 1914 in Lwow, Poland. She received her B.A. in psychology from York College in 1978 and her M.A. in creative writing from Queens College in 1983. A retired administrative assistant from the CUNY Graduate School, she currently teaches poetry and prose at a senior citizens' center in Queens, New York. Her short stories and poems have been published in numerous literary journals and anthologies including *The Poet Peu a Peu*, *American Poetry Anthology*, and *Hearts on Fire: A Treasury of Love Poems*.

JACK HAND studied writing at the Iowa Writer's Workshop and received his Ph.D. in American literature from Kent State University in 1971. His poetry has been published in *The Missouri Review*, *Yarrow*, *The Cumberland Review*, and *Three Rivers Poetry Journal*. In addition to poetry, he has written a novel, *At the End of the World Bazaar*. He taught creative writing at Columbia College in Missouri until his death on August 1, 1983.

EDWARD L. HOOPER lives in Peru, Illinois, with Cindy, his wife, and Stacy and Shani, their two children. Hooper first became interested in writing in 1968 while stationed in Vietnam, but following an automobile accident in 1978, his commitment to writing deepened. In 1981, he returned to Illinois Valley Community College and received his Associate of Arts degree. He has recently begun writing essays in the field of disability studies, and he has published poetry and prose in several journals, including *The Disability Rag*, *Disabled USA*, *Mainstream*, and *Kaleidoscope*.

DEBORAH KENDRICK was born in 1950 in Toledo, Ohio, and first announced her intention to become a writer at the age of eight. As a blind student, however, she was openly discouraged by skeptical rehabilitation counselors. After graduating from the public school system—"I was mainstreamed," she observes wryly, "before that was . . . trendy"—she received her B.A. from Adrian College in Michigan and her M.A. in English literature from Kent State University. In addition to her work in rehabilitation and education of the visually impaired, she has recently returned to her early goal of becoming a writer. Since 1980, she has published a wide range of general-interest articles, editorials, poems, and reviews in numerous journals and newspapers in Cincinnati, Ohio, where she currently resides with Melinda and Sean, her two children. Her work has also appeared in national journals, including *The Catholic Digest, Disabled USA,* and *Kaleidoscope.* In 1983, she received the Ned E. Freeman Writing Competition award sponsored by the American Council of the Blind.

NORMAN ANDREW KIRK, a resident of Dobbs Ferry, New York, has published his poems in many journals, including *The Atlantic Monthly, Poet Lore,* and *Bitterroot.* His work was recently included in *Friendship Bridge,* an anthology of one hundred American poets published in India. In 1983, following the publication of his first volume of poetry, he established his own publishing firm, West of Boston, in joint venture with *Bitterroot* magazine. His second volume of poetry, *Panda Zoo,* was the first publication of his firm.

NEIL MARCUS was born in New York City in 1954, and is currently a resident of Berkeley, California, where he serves as editor of a wry and informal journal, *Special Effects.* His writing includes prose as well as poetry, and he has recently completed a short story entitled "The Soul of a Wheelchair." He refers to himself as the "Buckminster Fuller of disability," noting his most recent interest as "breaking into standup comedy."

GLORIA MAXSON, a native of Minneapolis, lives in Whittier, California, with Charles, her husband, whom she met in the Mojave Desert during her first teaching assignment.

She graduated from UCLA in 1949 with a major in English and education. In 1983, she was honored as Writer of the Year by the Writer's Club of Whittier. She has also served as editor for the magazine *New World*, published by the California Association for the Physically Handicapped. A prolific writer, she has recently published poetry in the *Reader's Digest*, *Christian Century*, *Rational Review*, and *Living Church*. She has also published several volumes of poetry, ranging in scope from haiku to sonnets to five-line character sketches, which she calls "kennings." Her robot limericks, which she calls "Glorobots," have appeared in several computer and science journals.

VASSAR MILLER was born in 1924 in Houston, Texas, where she has lived all of her life. She received her B.A. and M.A. degrees in English from the University of Houston. A teacher of creative writing at St. John's School, she has also served as writer-in-residence at the University of St. Thomas. Her poetry has been published in hundreds of periodicals in the United States and Latin America, and in numerous anthologies. In addition, she has published seven volumes of poetry, three of which have won the annual poetry prize of the Texas Institute of Letters. Her poetry was also distinguished by nomination for the Pulitzer Prize in Poetry in 1961. Her latest book of poetry is entitled *Selected and New Poems, 1950–1980*, and she has recently edited *Despite This Flesh*, an anthology of poetry and prose that explores the experiences of disability.

JANICE TOWNLEY MOORE was born in Atlanta, Georgia, in 1939, and lives in the mountains of northern Georgia, where she teaches English at Young Harris College and serves as poetry editor for the *Georgia Journal.* She received her B.A. from LaGrange College and her M.A. from Auburn University. She has also studied at the University of Virginia, Emory University, and Georgia State University. Her poetry has been widely published in literary journals, including *Southern Poetry Review*, *Negative Capabilities*, and *Southern Humanities Review.* Her work has also been represented in several issues of the *Anthology of Magazine Verse and Yearbook of American Poetry* and most recently in *Light Year '85*, an anthology published at Case Western Reserve University.

LILLIAN MORRISON was born in New Jersey in 1917, and is currently a resident of New York City, where she serves as poetry editor for the *Film Library Quarterly.* She received her B.S. in mathematics from Douglass College (Rutgers University) and her M.A. in library service from Columbia University. Until her retirement in 1982, she was the Coordinator of Young Adult Services for the New York Public Library. She is the author of six volumes of poetry, the most recent of which, *The Break Dance Kids*, was published in 1985. Her poetry has appeared in many periodicals and anthologies, including *The Atlantic Monthly*, *Poetry Northwest*, *The Croton Review*, and *Light Year.*

DIXIE PARTRIDGE was born in 1943 and grew up in western Wyoming on a small farm settled by her great-grandfather. The mother of six children, she and her family currently reside in Richland, Washington. In 1965, she received her B.A. in English from Brigham Young University. In recent years, she has been the recipient of the William Stafford Award in Writing and has published poetry in a number of periodicals, including

Sunstone, *The Montana Review*, and *Quarterly West*. Her first book of poetry, *Deer in the Haystacks*, was published in 1984.

FELIX POLLAK, a native of Vienna, Austria, came to the United States in 1938, a refugee from Hitler's Third Reich. He and his wife are currently residents of Madison, Wisconsin. He holds his Doctor of Juriprudence degree from the University of Vienna and his M.A. in library science from the University of Michigan. Following his service in the United States Army during World War II, he became the curator of special collections at Northwestern University Library. From 1959 to 1974, he served as curator of rare books at the University of Wisconsin in Madison, until failing eyesight led to his early retirement. His translations of German poetry have appeared recently in *American Poetry Review*, *Northwest Review*, *Triquarterly*, and *Literary Review*. He has also published a volume of prose and five volumes of poetry, the most recent of which, *Tunnel Visions*, was published in 1984.

ROBIN GATHANY SHEA was born in 1958 in Lake Forest, Illinois. She currently lives in Lowell, Massachusetts, with Kevin, her husband, and their child. They are expecting their second child in February of 1986. In 1980, she earned her B.A. in English and French at Colby College in Waterville, Maine. Following college, she spent a year as a Vista volunteer, working for Prime Movers and the Center for Accessible Living, disability rights organizations in Louisville, Kentucky. She has also worked with emotionally disturbed children in a local residential treatment center.

SHARON A. STERN was born in 1943 in Brooklyn, New York, and currently lives on Roosevelt Island with Kiwi, her cat. Having been, as she says, "more athletic than scholarly" in her youth, she traces her interest in the arts, especially literature, to her disability, which occurred at nine years of age. In 1976, she received her B.A. in the humanities from Empire State College. In addition to writing poetry, her special interests are reading, writing, editing, and "worshipping the sun."

LAURIE STROBLAS, born in Manhattan in 1948, is a resident of Washington, D.C., where she teaches creative writing at the Filmore Arts Center. Majoring in English, she earned her B.A. from SUNY and her M.A. from the University of Massachusetts. The recipient of the Larry Neal Writer's Conference Poetry Award in 1984 and the D.C. Commission on the Arts Fellowship in 1984 and 1985, she has published her poetry in numerous literary magazines and anthologies, including *Poet Lore*, *Negative Capabilities*, *Greenfield Review*, and the *Anthology of Magazine Verse and Yearbook of American Poetry*. She has read her poetry, with corresponding sign language, at the Folger Shakespeare Library's Midday Muse Series and other D.C. area cultural events.

CONSTANCE E. STUDER, who resides in Boulder, Colorado, earned her M.A. in English and creative writing from the University of Colorado and her nursing diploma from the Toledo Hospital School of Nursing in Ohio. In addition to her publications in professional nursing journals, she currently serves as editor of *The Pulse*, a newsletter for nurses at Boulder Community Hospital. Her poetry has been published in literary journals and anthologies, including *Pegasus*, *Hyperion*, and *Womanthology*. She has also published translations of Dutch poetry in *Practices of the Wind* and *Blue Buildings*.

AMBER COVERDALE SUMRALL was born in 1945 and lives in the Santa Cruz Mountains with her husband and seven cats. Her poetry has appeared in *Matrix*, *Womanspirit*, and *Sinister Wisdom*, and her autobiographical short story, "A Leg to Stand On," was recently published in *With the Power of Each Breath*, an anthology of prose by women with disabilities. She is currently at work editing an anthology of erotic writings by women.

EVELYN THOMAS was born in rural Mineola, New York, near Manhattan. Her childhood combined the advantages of a small-town identity with the cultural diversity of New York City, which she calls her "Pleasure Dome." Encouraged by family and teachers, she recalls the ease and spontaneity of her early writing. She received her B.A. in art and music from the University of Missouri in 1944, and her M.A. in library science from Florida State University in 1958. Currently retired because of complications from rheumatoid arthritis, she has worked as a librarian in many places, including Lima, Peru, where she served as Director of Libraries. She has also been a television commentator, society reporter, university professor, free-lance medical science writer, and political activist. In the latter capacity, she assisted in writing the plank on disability at the Democratic Convention in Florida near her current home in West Palm Beach.

JAMES WEIGEL, JR., was born in Cleveland, Ohio, in 1937, and currently lives in Marshalltown, Iowa. In 1959, he received his B.A. in history with a minor in English from Wayne State University, and later earned graduate credit at Indiana University's School of Letters. The scope of his writing is wide-ranging, including book reviews for *Time Magazine* and several major newspapers, as well as extensive scholarly work for *Masterplots* and the Cliff's Notes series. His poetry has been published in the *Minnesota Review*, *Blue Heron*, and *Heron Review*. Seven of his poems are featured in a private, limited-edition art book, *Thresholds*, created and illustrated by Chicago artist Maralyn Dettman. *Celebrations*, his most recent volume of poetry, was published in 1984. He recently served as the Ballenger Chair Poet at Mott Community College in Michigan and as the Mastodon Live Poet at Moraine Valley Community College in Illinois.

ZANA was born in 1947 and currently lives in rural Arizona, near Tucson. A writer and an artist, she has published her work widely in the feminist press, and has recently published *herb womon*, a collection of her poetry and drawings. In addition to the arts, her interests include methods of natural self-healing and the discovery of positive ways of interdependent group living.

Select Bibliography

Bower, Eli M., ed. *The Handicapped in Literature: A Psychosocial Perspective*. Denver/London: Love Publishing Co., 1980.

Brightman, Alan J., ed. *Ordinary Moments*. Baltimore: University Park Press, 1984.

Brown, Christy. *My Left Foot: The Story of Christy Brown*. New York: Simon & Schuster, 1954.

———. *Down All the Days*. New York: Stein & Day, 1970.

Brown, Susan, Debra Connors, and Nanci Stern, eds. *With the Power of Each Breath: A Disabled Woman's Anthology*. Pittsburg/San Francisco: Cleis Press, 1985.

Carrillo, Ann Cupolo, Katherine Corbett, and Victoria Lewis, devs. *No More Stares*. Berkeley: The Disability Rights Education and Defense Fund, 1982.

Kirk, Norman Andrew. *Some Poems, My Friends*. Boston: Four Zoas Night House, 1981.

———. *Panda Zoo*. Wayland, Mass.: Bitterroot, 1983.

Krents, Harold. *To Race The Wind*. Elsevier, N.Y.: Dutton Publishing Co., 1972.

Kriegel, Leonard. *The Long Walk Home*. East Norwalk, Ct.: Appleton-Century, 1964.

Miller, Vassar, ed. *Despite This Flesh: The Disabled in Stories and Poems*. Austin: University of Texas Press, 1985.

Pity and Fear: Myths and Images of the Disabled in Literature Old and New. New York: International Center for the Disabled, 1981. Collection of papers from symposium held in New York City in 1981.

Pollak, Felix. *Tunnel Visions*. Peoria, Ill.: Spoon River Poetry Press, 1984.

Potak, Andrew. *Ordinary Daylight*. New York: Holt, Rinehart & Winston, 1980.

Sheed, Wilfred. *People Will Always Be Kind*. New York: Farrar, Straus and Giroux, 1973.

———. "On Being Handicapped," *Newsweek*, August 25, 1980, p. 13.

Sutherland, Alan T. *Disabled We Stand*. Bloomington: Indiana University Press, 1984.

Warfield, Frances. *Cotton in My Ears*. New York: Curtis, 1948.

Zingale, Jeanne W. "The Disabled as Taboo: An Examination of Physically Disabled Characters in Twentieth Century Plays Produced in New York City." Ph.D. dissertation, Kent State University, 1984.

Zola, Irving Kenneth, ed. *Ordinary Lives: Voices of Disability and Disease*. Cambridge, Mass./Watertown: Apple-wood Books, 1982.

For specific commentary on the poetry in this anthology, see:

Baird, J. L. "En-Abled Poetry," *Kaleidoscope* 7 (1983): 33–35. Reprinted in *Mainstream* 8, no. 12 (1983): 14–16, and *Rehabilitation Digest* 14 (1983): 15–17.

———. "Breathing New Winds," *Disabled USA* 2 (1984): 19–22.

———. "New Spirit of Disability Surfaces through Poetry," *Mainstream* 10, no. 12 (1985): 9–11.

Author-Title Index

"Adjustments," 114
"Angles," 21
"Arthritis," 29
Astrachan, John Mann, 42
"At Nuclear Medicine," 23
"At the National Air and Space Museum," 68

Bachstein, Michael, 38
Beckerman, H. N., 113
"bitter herbs," 46
"Black Aggie," 57
Bond, Harold, 25
"broken," 107

"Capes," 98
"'Caught behind words . . . ,'" 60
"Changeling, The," 50
Cleary, Michael, 112
"Clinics," 38
Colvin, Norma Thomas, 75
"Covering All Bases," 99
"Cowboy-Boot Sale," 76
Crago, William D., 115
"Crip," 57
"Cripple in Sight," 67
Crosson, John, 67

"Dancing on Water," 26
Davis, Marilyn, 49

Davis, Nedine, 37
"Death Stairs/Life House," 101
"Detour," 27
"Disabled Calligraphy," 66
"'Don't smile . . . ,'" 61
"Dramatic Monologue in the Speaker's Own Voice," 119
Dunn, Susan L., 32

"Earthquake Somewhere Else, An," 81
"Enid Field: In Memoriam," 62

"Farewell, A," 17
Finch, Vivienne, 77
"Finger, The," 125
"Fingers, Fists, Gabriel's Wings," 112
"For Mama," 92
Friedman, S. L., 30

"Game, The," 25
Gaumond, Mary R., 18
Glading, Jan, 29
Goldsmith, Frederica, 98

Hand, Jack, 100
Hooper, Edward L., 52
"How to Sign," 97

"I Am Mama Bear," 37

"I Know, You'd Rather Be Dead," 52
"Incident," 127

"Jenny," 42
"Journey, The," 77

Kendrick, Deborah, 92
Kirk, Norman Andrew, 57
"kol nidre," 45

Marcus, Neil, 65
Maxson, Gloria, 62
"Me and Hercule Poirot," 94
Miller, Vassar, 116
"Mirage," 109
Moore, Janice Townley, 68
Morrison, Lillian, 43
"My Name in the Star Registry," 40

"On Being Stone," 79
"On Forgetting to Cry," 75
"On Seeing a Construction of a Sheet Metal Man," 30
"On the Sidelines," 43

"Pain," 104
"Pain Is My Brother," 100
Partridge, Dixie, 21
Pollak, Felix, 121

"Question of Art, A," 93
"Question of Energy, A," 108
"Questions," 110

"Reality," 121
"reawakening," 44
"Reflections," 69
"Rose, The," 19

"Sampson," 117
Shea, Robin Gathany, 60
"Song for My Son," 49
"Spastic Child," 117
Stern, Sharon A., 44
Stroblas, Laurie, 97
Studer, Constance E., 69
"Subterfuge," 116
Sumrall, Amber Coverdale, 108
"Suspension," 70

"talisman 18," 48
"Terms of Surrender," 39
"Testament I," 13
"Testament V," 14
"Testament XXVI," 15
"Testament XXVIII," 16
"Testament XXX," 16
"'They are all too kind . . . ,'" 33
Thomas, Evelyn, 99
"Tingle, The," 58
"'Today, again, the jagged black line . . . ,'" 32
"'Tonight I stood looking . . . ,'" 32
"'To: The Access Committee . . . ,'" 113
"Tunnel Visions," 123
"Two Guitars," 63

"'Virus Poliomyelitis,'" 18

"Way Downtown, The," 53
Weigel, James, Jr., 13
"'. . . where late the sweet birds sang,'" 115
"While Pruning," 22

zana, 107
"'Zotz!,'" 65

Index of First Lines

A B C D E F G, 66
A mouth should launch words
    gracefully, 16
An agile voice, quick smile, and
    leaping eyes, 62
As if in that far Pentecostal
    day, 63
A silk of flame composed his
    hair to fleck, 117
A wooden puppet with tangled, 49

Beyond, 76
bitter herbs, 46

Caught behind words, 60

damn, 29
Darkly in vesper stillness, 81
Dawn peeled mists, 19
Don't smile, 61

First the light cracked, 123

Gram died with most of her
    joints frozen, 21

Hallway whispers still echo, 52

I could say that, 115
i don't cry because it was my
    favorite glass, 107

If I ransom my injuries, 43
I know you'd do anything for
    me, 114
I look out my window at night,
    125
'i missed you at services last
    night,' 45
I'm not diminished, 108
Invent and *father* are said at the
    forehead, 97
I remember my father, slight,
    116
I should quit this craft, 15
It's all a blur of speed, 70
I walk naked under my clothes
    like anyone else, 119

Lazarus-like, I am restored, 99
Like an army of locusts, 69
Like something very precious,
    he holds it in his hands, 93

Mama never rocked me, 92
Mothers who clutch the hands
    of your children, 26
My body fell asleep years ago.
    Cut off, 58
My bootheels and my cane, 101
My voice, plucked from the air,
    112

on the sidewalk, 53
Out of my sleeves ten bones protrude, 16

Pain is my brother, 100
People always tell me things, 94

Rigid in their dead man's stare, 67

Sampson sulking in his cell regretted his, 117
Strange how, 75

The accident, 109
The bank foyer is plush. People pass, 127
The egg grew human, 13
The old german nurse, 44
There is a long journey to be made, 77
The road was straight up to the last, 27
These two, dissimilar, understood, 104
The silver Spirit of St. Louis, 68
The streets are full of people moving, 121
The whisper was recorded and rehearsed, 57
They are all too kind, 33
They have met here before: five old women, 23
They stare, 110

They swathed me in, 98
To bear the label of disabled is as dull, 57
Today, again, the jagged black line, 32
Tonight I stood looking, 32
To: The Access Committee, 113
Translated once, 14

Unhappy childhood, please do not curve, 39

Watching me approach, Goldilocks asks, 37
What does it mean, 50
What it is to be stone, 79
What tree would shape itself like this?, 22
When I am four a crippled hospital, 38
While time hustled, 17
With my luck, 40

You are my friends. You do things, 25
Your words haunt me in the night, 48
You see it's that she can't remember songs, 42
You sent me, God, 18
You tell me somewhere, 30

Zotz!!! You n*ame,it.kind of n.e.w. thing.EMERGing, 65

Thematic Index

Aging: "Testament I," 13; "The Rose," 19; "While Pruning," 22; "Angles," 21; "Two Guitars," 63; "Reflections," 69

Alienation: "Testament V," 14; "On Seeing a Construction of a Sheet Metal Man," 30; "Clinics," 38; "Terms of Surrender," 39; "reawakening," 44; "kol nidre," 45; "Black Aggie," 57; "Cripple in Sight," 67; "On Being Stone," 79; "An Earthquake Somewhere Else," 81; "A Question of Art," 93; "Me and Hercule Poirot," 94; "Capes," 98; ". . . where late the sweet birds sang," 115; "Spastic Child," 117; "Dramatic Monologue in the Speaker's Own Voice," 119; "Tunnel Visions," 123; "The Finger," 125

Anger: "The Game," 25; "'Today, again, the jagged black line . . . ,'" 32; "'They are all too kind . . . ,'" 33; "bitter herbs," 46; "I Know, You'd Rather Be Dead," 52; "'Caught behind words . . . ,'" 60; "'Don't smile . . . ,'" 61; "Cripple in Sight," 67; "Sampson," 117; "Dramatic Monologue in the Speaker's Own Voice," 119

Art and writing: "Testament XXVI," 15; "Testament XXVIII," 16; "My Name in the Star Registry," 40; "On the Sidelines," 43; "Disabled Calligraphy," 66; "Pain," 104; "Fingers, Fists, Gabriel's Wings," 112; "Subterfuge," 116

Barriers: "Dancing on Water," 26; "The Way Downtown," 53; "Reflections," 69; "The Journey," 77; "broken," 107; "Questions," 110

Bemused detachment: "'Virus Poliomyelitis,'" 18; "Crip," 57; "Me and Hercule Poirot," 94

Blindness: "'Tonight I stood looking . . . ,'" 32; "'Today, again, the jagged black line . . . ,'" 32; "'They are all too kind . . . ,'" 33; "For Mama," 92; "A Question of Art," 93; "Adjustments,"

114; "Sampson," 117; "Reality," 121; "Tunnel Visions," 123; "The Finger," 125; "Incident," 127

Childhood reflections: "Angles," 21; "Clinics," 38; "Terms of Surrender," 39; "For Mama," 92; "Capes," 98; "Subterfuge," 116; "Incident," 127

Child's view: "I Am Mama Bear," 37

Communication: "Testament XXX," 16; "Zotz!," 65; "On Being Stone," 79; "How to Sign," 97; "Fingers, Fists, Gabriel's Wings," 112; "Adjustments," 114; "Spastic Child," 117

Day-to-day realities: "The Game," 25; "I Am Mama Bear," 37; "The Way Downtown," 53; "On Forgetting to Cry," 75; "Cowboy-Boot Sale," 76; "The Journey," 77; "broken," 107; "Questions," 110; "Adjustments," 114; "Incident," 127

Deafness: "How to Sign," 97; "Fingers, Fists, Gabriel's Wings," 112

Death: "Testament I," 13; "A Farewell," 17; "While Pruning," 22; "talisman 18," 48; "I Know, You'd Rather Be Dead," 52; "Two Guitars," 63; "Reflections," 69; "Pain Is My Brother," 100; "Death Stairs/Life House," 101; "Dramatic Monologue in the Speaker's Own Voice,"119

Desire: "Testament V," 14; "Black Aggie," 57; "Mirage," 109; "Dramatic Monologue in the Speaker's Own Voice," 119

Fear: "'Today, again, the jagged black line . . . ,'" 32; "Clinics," 38; "The Tingle," 58; "Suspension," 70; "An Earthquake Somewhere Else," 81; "A Question of Art," 93

Humor: "My Name in the Star Registry," 40; "Disabled Calligraphy," 66; "Covering All Bases," 99; "'To: The Access Committee . . . ,'" 113

Irony: "Testament XXVI," 15; "'Virus Poliomyelitis,'" 18; "The Game," 25; "Arthritis," 29; "On Seeing a Construction of a Sheet Metal Man," 30; "'They are all too kind . . . ,'" 33; "My Name in the Star Registry," 40; "I Know, You'd Rather Be Dead," 52; "Crip," 57; "Disabled Calligraphy," 66; "Me and Hercule Poirot," 94; "A Question of Energy," 108; "Adjustments," 114; "Reality," 121; "Incident," 127

Pain: "While Pruning," 22; "Arthritis," 29; "The Tingle," 58; "Suspension," 70; "On Being Stone," 79; "An Earthquake Somewhere Else," 81; "Pain Is My Brother," 100; "Death Stairs/Life House," 101; "Pain," 104

Parent and child: "Jenny," 42; "Song for My Son," 49; "The Changeling," 50; "For Mama," 92

Relationships: "Testament XXX," 16; "The Rose," 19; "Detour," 27; "On the Sidelines," 43; "Two Guitars," 63; "Cowboy-Boot Sale," 76; "A Question of Art," 93; "Me and Hercule Poirot," 94; "Mirage," 109; "Adjustments," 114

Synthesis: "Testament I," 13; "Testament V," 14; "Testament XXVIII," 16; "Testament XXX," 16; "'Virus Poliomyelitis,'" 18; "Dancing on Water," 26; "'Tonight I stood looking . . . ,'" 32; "Terms of Surrender," 39; "On the Sidelines," 43; "re-awakening," 44; "kol nidre," 45; "Black Aggie," 57; "Enid Field: In Memoriam," 62; "Zotz!," 65; "At the National Air and Space Museum," 68; "On Forgetting to Cry," 75; "Cowboy-Boot Sale," 76; "The Journey," 77; "For Mama," 92; "How to Sign," 97; "A Question of Energy," 108; "Sampson," 117

Technology: "At Nuclear Medicine," 23; "On Seeing a Construction of a Sheet Metal Man," 30; "At the National Air and Space Museum," 68; "An Earthquake Somewhere Else," 81